Those who read Farther In and Deeper Down *will be profoundly challenged and invigorated. E.K. knows the context of the Scriptures and makes present-tense application for those who walk with the Father and have personal fellowship with the Son.*
Melvin V. Wade, Sr.
> Pastor, Mt. Moriah Missionary Baptist Church
> President, National Missionary
> Baptist Convention of America

Wherever you are on your spiritual journey, Farther In and Deeper Down *will provide guidance and hope for times of struggle and challenge. This book provides a window into how the heart of God colors our world with love and direction when we feel like life is crashing in on us. A valuable resource for you personally and for ministry to those you love.*
> Larry A. Mercer,
> President, Washington Bible College/Capital Bible Seminary

The life, the ministry, and the preaching of Dr. E. K. Bailey took people farther in and deeper down. If you want truth for tough times, this book will be an incredible blessing. This book blends the Bible and E. K. Bailey himself as truth and experience are fused together. Such incarnational instruction leads to redemptive and transforming results.
> David L. Olford
> President, Olford Ministries International

E. K. Bailey is at his best in this awe-inspiring book. This pastor/scholar pairs the biblical texts with the complexities and uncertainties of life in a manner commensurate to his years of wisdom and maturity. Every page is filled with hope for all who come asking, "Watchman, what of the night? Is there a word from the Lord?"
> Cleophus J. LaRue
> Patton Associate Professor of Homiletics, Princeton
> Theological Seminary

As a pastor and a counselor for forty years, I have observed that the majority of Christians do not suffer well. This book teaches how to know how to suffer well. Dr. E. K. Bailey models for us how to keep God in the center of our existence as we walk through the valley of the shadow of death.
> Willie Richardson
> Pastor, Christian Stronghold Baptist Church

Mrs. Bailey and Cokiesha have done an extraordinary labor of love in putting together Dr. Bailey's words and thoughts. This book is a must-read for anyone who is suffering, or who loves someone who is suffering.

Denise George
Author, teacher, speaker

It's not the crossing of that final river that intrigues me, for the mists too much obscure the real and distant other side. It's the certainty with which all discussions end and our last words are "I'll be seeing you," and we release a friend to sail alone across the bright waters of faith. This is the final tale of joy—the account of a family on the banks of foreverness, kissing illusion good-bye, so reality can take its eternal turn at life.

Calvin Miller
Professor of Divinity, Beeson Divinity School

Every pastor needs a pastor—Dr. E. K. Bailey was mine. He preached for me, prayed for me, and was the presence of Jesus to me. He walked through the deepest valleys and darkest shadows of life, and brought us all closer to his Father. As you share his journey, you'll find his joy.

Jim Denison
Senior Pastor, Park Cities Baptist Church, Dallas, Texas

Farther In and Deeper Down *is a profound testimonial of God's sovereign capacity to transform our lives even through such deadly situations as cancer.*

Bryan Carter
Senior Pastor, Concord Baptist Church

Pastor E. K. Bailey, along with his wife, Sheila, and daughter Cokiesha, have written a book that every patient with cancer should read. This book is about deepening one's relationship with Christ through the experiences of adversity involved with cancer. If cancer is your "thorn in the flesh", you must read this book so that God may take you Farther In and Deeper Down.

Wm. Lee Cowden, M.D.

Farther In
And Deeper Down

E. K. BAILEY
with SHEILA M. BAILEY
and COKIESHA L. BAILEY

MOODY PUBLISHERS
CHICAGO

All Scripture quotations, unless otherwise indicated, are taken from the *New American Standard Bible*®, Copyright © The Lockman Foundation 1960, 1962, 1963, 1968, 1971, 1972, 1973, 1975, 1977, 1995. Used by permission.

Scripture quotations marked NIV are taken from the *Holy Bible, New International Version*®. NIV®. Copyright © 1973, 1978, 1984 by International Bible Society. Used by permission of Zondervan Publishing House. All rights reserved.

Scripture quotations marked KJV are taken from the King James Version.

Library of Congress Cataloging-in-Publication Data

Bailey, E. K.
    Farther in and deeper down / E.K. Bailey ; with Sheila M. Bailey And Cokiesha L. Bailey.
        p. cm.
    ISBN-10: 0-8024-5401-1
    ISBN-13: 978-0-8024-5401-0
        1. Consolation. 2. Cancer--Patients—Religious life. 3. Cancer—Religious aspects—Christianity. 4. Bailey, E. K., 1945- I. Bailey, Sheila M. II. Bailey, Cokiesha L. III. Title.

    BV4910.33.B35 2005
    248.8'6196994'0092—dc22

                                                                2005003986

ISBN: 0-8024-5401-1
ISBN-13: 978-0-8024-5401-0

1 3 5 7 9 10 8 6 4 2

Printed in the United States of America

CONTENTS

FOREWORD

I met E. K. Bailey for the first time in the lobby of Le Meriden Hotel in Dallas. As the host of the 1998 International Conference on Expository Preaching, Dr. Bailey was serving as the official greeter as well. I can still see him warmly interacting with everyone. Like Ezekiel, he sat where they were sitting (Ezekiel 3:15).

Oftentimes our expressions exceed our experience. Not here. After being diagnosed with nasal cancer, he wrote in the *Dallas Morning News*, "Now I must preach with my life." From that time I noticed that the smell of every text he preached was heavily upon him.

In this book E. K. Bailey not only takes us to the banquet table where his cup runs over, he also takes us through the valley of the shadow of death where he experiences the accompanying presence of the Lord. E. K. Bailey could announce with unswerving confidence and unshakable conviction that "God causes all things to work together for good to those who love God, to those who are called according to His purpose" (Romans 8:28). This was one of E. K. Bailey's favorite texts.

This work serves as a personal handbook for cancer patients, their families, counselors, advocates, and beginning and experienced ministers, because E. K. Bailey was always going farther in and deeper down in *exegesis* and *experience*. This challenges us to not only grapple with the what question of the text but also the *so what* and *now what* question of everyday living. He was always going farther in and deeper down in connecting the head and heart because he knew that he could not afford to feed the mind and neglect the heart.

He was effective in adapting his presentation to an audience of any race or culture without compromising the message of the gospel. This is the pulsating heartbeat felt in a book that he coauthored with Dr. Warren W. Wiersbe, entitled *Preaching in Black and White*.

The great Greek playwright Aeschylus wrote, "In our sleep, pain which cannot be forgotten falls drop by drop upon the heart, until in our own despair, against our will, comes wisdom through the awful grace of God." These words are embodied by Dr. E. K. Bailey and are expressed in this book.

Everyone who reads *Farther In and Deeper Down* can expect to discover much more of the inexhaustible riches of Christ, for E. K. Bailey's greatest aspiration was not to know more but to know Him—"That I may know Him and the power of His resurrection and the fellowship of His sufferings" (Philippians 3:10).

ROBERT SMITH
Professor of Preaching,
Beeson Divinity School

INTRODUCTION
Farther In . . . Deeper Down

*T*here once was a farmer who hired a worker to dig a well on his farm. They agreed that the cost of the well would be determined by its depth. Nine feet down he hit water. The well-digger told the farmer that the well would last for a good many years.

The farmer then asked, "Will this well be deep enough to make it through the dry seasons?"

"No, this is just for normal rain," the well-digger replied. "When the dry seasons comes, it won't be deep enough to bring you water."

"Keep on digging," the farmer said. "I don't care how much it costs; it needs to be deeper."

So they kept digging until at thirty feet they hit a wellspring.

"Good," the farmer said. "You've gone farther in and deeper down. I'll pay the price for a well that can handle dry seasons."

The primary reason that I write this book is to tell cancer patients, our loved ones, and our caregivers that we need a well that can handle dry seasons. We need to dig down deep and go farther in. If we stay on the surface, we will be shallow our whole lives, and when the winds of adversity blow, we'll be swept away. But if we keep on digging—digging into the Word of God, digging into our prayer lives, digging into blessing other people—when the dry season comes, we'll have a wellspring of life and joy coming from a very deep well.

If you are in the midst of a dry season, like dealing with a major illness, you especially need a deep well. The patients who draw on the wellspring of life in Christ Jesus find that He is enough to cope with their condition, boost their spirits, and better their quality of life. Studies have proven that people exhibiting faith in God live longer than those who do not. But when resentment and anger block faith and hope, people dry up and blow away.

But even Christians falter in crisis. I have a friend who truly loves God, but since he has been battling cancer he doesn't pray anymore. Other Christian patients have questioned how God could allow them to suffer.

I have played my own game of spiritual "tug-of-war" while battling cancer three different times. But even on a day when I am feeling my worst, God assures me that He loves me deeply. When the shock of a diagnosis has worn off and the dust settles, I am certain of God's goodness and His grace. What has been the difference? I hope you discover in these snapshots of my experience that peace has come after my choice to trust God at all costs.

I pray that this book will help you concentrate on the character of God during life's most difficult moments. I want patients, their family network, caregivers, and friends to be reminded that despite health challenges, God never abandons us. I encourage you to enter a new relationship with God. My prayer is that starting today you will encounter His peace, provision, and providence in a fresh way. God's Word promises you that He has plans for His children. Knowing that He will remain faithful to His promise, I urge you to remain faithful to Him.

It would be so easy for me to tell you to take my word for it, but my word isn't good enough. I will encourage you instead to look at how Jesus kept digging as He headed to Calvary. He knew that there was no other rescue that would be deep enough, so He kept on digging. He dug until He hit redemption. He dug till He hit salvation. He dug till He hit justification. He kept on digging. He dug till He hit a second chance. He dug till He hit mercy. He dug till He hit grace. He dug until He closed His eyes and bowed His head and died for you and me. Then God said, "That's deep enough!"

A few summers ago my friend Robert Smith preached at our Expository Preaching Conference. God used Dr. Smith to specifically speak to many needs on that day. As I sat there lapping up his message, I found myself arrested by the title, "Farther In and Deeper Down." That title resonated in my mind and exploded in my heart. That is it! That is what God has called me to do, here and now, with cancer and uncertain about the days ahead.

Perhaps your physical condition or that of a loved one has eclipsed your vision of God's promises. If so, then I'm glad that you're joining me on a journey that is sure to change your perspective on illness, suffering, and death. There are treasures lying beneath the surface of your life that you can only discover as you go farther in and deeper down.

If you are willing to allow God to prove His character to you, please sign the agreement below. May it serve as a daily reminder of your commitment to trust Him even in the dry seasons.

Your name _____

Date _____

That we may know Him,
E. K. BAILEY

And we know

that God causes

all things to work together

for good to those

who love God,

to those who are called

according to His purpose.

–Romans 8:28

Chapter 1

GOD RESCUES US WITH HIS GOODNESS

Delivered and Directed at Seventeen

*H*ave you ever needed to be rescued? Yes, *rescued.*

Have you ever needed to be snatched out of an overwhelming situation? Have you ever prayed for deliverance when it seemed like the walls were caving in on you? When was the last time you needed to be taken out of harm's way? I am sure you have been there at least once.

All of us have faced situations that seemed dark, desperate, and desolate. Each of us has prayed to be taken from death's door to a safe haven of peace and restoration.

If I'm not mistaken, all of us have also been at a place where we have pleaded with God to save us spiritually, mentally, or emotionally.

"Please, God, mend my broken heart."

"Please, God, deliver me from this situation."

"Please, God, I have no one to turn to but You."

Desperate circumstances cause us to cry out to the Lord for help.

It is in these times that we need a spiritual revival. In these desperate moments, we need God's strength to revive us from a code-blue situation. At these times more than any other, we need the One who can capture us and rescue us from our own fears, our insecurities, our own warped way of thinking, or our own painful pasts.

Are you facing that kind of desperate circumstance today? Let your faith be stirred by the evidence that God hears and God delivers.

"IT'S NOT FAIR!"

I was seventeen the first time I felt this kind of desperation. My father was buried not too much longer after the country mourned the loss of our esteemed President John F. Kennedy. I remember wearing sadness like a winter coat . . . my heart was so heavy. My parents had divorced when I was much younger, and I had chosen to live with my dad. His new wife had never taken to me but had tolerated me only as her husband's son. Needless to say, shortly after my father's funeral she kicked me out of the house.

For days I wandered the streets of Oakland with no money and no place to go. I felt abandoned and alone. My heart and my mind played tug-of-war. I told myself, *You can get over this, E.K. When life gives you lemons, just make some lemonade. Right?* Yeah, right. That would be some sour lemonade.

I wanted to be depressed. "It's not fair!" I shouted. I was guest of honor at my own pity party. Over and over I asked myself, *How would a young black man get a new start without the guidance, wisdom, and protection of his father? Why would God do this to me?*

My father had left a rich legacy. He was an outstanding orator, a prolific and powerful preacher. He was tall, well-groomed, and dedicated to preaching the truth of Christ. He was the rock of our family, and I adored him. How could his life be so tragically snatched away? What would become of me? Even if I made a name for myself, my father would never be able to see me reach my goals. I remember sitting on a park bench one night, looking at the sky and getting angrier by the second. Not only did I feel fatherless, but I felt hopeless.

Then I began to hear God assuring me of His presence. I sensed Him drawing me close to Him, whispering, "When I take, I never take all." I began to cry because I knew that

I must work my way through the pain. I had to concentrate on what God had left me: my father's rich legacy, a healthy body, a creative mind, a long list of goals and dreams, a mother who loved me, supportive siblings, and caring friends. In my desperation I had forgotten about all the people miles away who were praying for me and rooting for my success. Little did I realize that God was quietly working behind the scenes to prepare even more encouraging people to enter my life.

Most of all, it was in those days of desperation that I discovered that God had left me the gift of His comfort and unconditional love. I drew from the strength and example of my ancestors, who continued to plow and pray despite their exploitation, tears, and bloodshed. I had to press on because my father, the late Reverend V. M. Bailey, would have wanted it that way. Sitting on that park bench, I decided that I would live as my father had, serving Jesus Christ.

RESCUED AT SEVENTEEN

With nowhere else to go that day, I went to the Lord.

I acknowledged my fears and my frustrations to Him and surrendered to His sovereign plan for my life. I cried harder as God dealt with me. I admitted to Him that I had been running for years from His call on my life to preach the gospel. Because my father served as a senior pastor for so many years, going to church was not an option for our family. When the doors were open, we were there. However, it wasn't until that dark night on the park bench that the love for God's church began to grow in me. Flooding my mind were all the Scriptures that I had learned, prayers that I had prayed, and sermons that I had heard over my lifetime. I began to be filled with an overwhelming and unbelievable amount of joy.

At my point of desperation, I remembered all the other times in my life when God had kept me, kept my family, kept my friends, kept my reputation, kept my mind, kept my body, and kept my feet from stumbling. Before I knew it, my tears of sadness turned into tears of joy.

God did it! He rescued me! He snatched me from the very jaws of death. He rescued me from my own selfish thoughts. God helped me to fight against the negative thoughts with which Satan had tried to suffocate me.

I dried my tears and praised God for His faithfulness and for His extravagant love. I worshiped Him right there in the park because God's greatness, goodness, and compassion were so much greater than my hurt.

God used the deep pain of that experience to dig a well of joy. I was certain that God would use me—not because I was smart enough or had enough money and certainly not because I was a Bailey but because He had plans for me. He had plans to prosper me and to give me a hope and a future (Jeremiah 29:11). Beginning then and there, I had an unquenchable desire to tell the world the good news of Jesus Christ. I was on a quest to search the Scriptures and share with the world the hope of a God who lives.

OFF TO COLLEGE

After the next several months of strengthening encouragement from good friends and my godfather, the late Rev. W. K. Jackson, I moved to Dallas to attend Bishop College. Throughout my schooling at Bishop, I felt God's hand move me from a state of depression to a state of adoration. Like the apostle Paul, I experienced a transformation. I went from being confused to being consecrated. No matter how much it hurt, I delighted to know God was smoothing out the ugly, rough edges of my life, shaping me into His image.

Now, more than three decades later, I see the value of hanging on at the end of the rope. Because of God's faithfulness, I have achieved my goals personally, academically, and professionally. I am so grateful to God that He has blessed me with a beautiful wife of thirty-four years and three loving children who also love the Lord. As a gift from the Lord, He has allowed me to serve as pastor of the Concord Church for almost thirty years. I am grateful to have been invited to preach and teach around the world. I thank God for an opportunity to tell of His goodness from the pulpit, from the pages of a book, or through conversation with a passing stranger.

HE ALWAYS DELIVERS

I see the importance of getting up after I have fallen down. I know without any doubt that God cannot use anyone greatly until He hurts him or her significantly. We cannot drink grapes until they have been crushed, and neither can we live out our full God-given potential until He has crushed us, emptied us, broken us, and burned out any trace of self. The good news is that *He always delivers!*

God may not answer our cry in the way we expect, but He always displays His glory in our personal experiences. He delights in rescuing us when we're floating downstream. God is loving and compassionate. Even when He allows us to endure pain, He strengthens, settles, and sustains us (1 Peter 5:10). Through His Word, His comfort, and His promises, I have been a front-row witness to how He secures our world with goodness. Everything that happens to us will not necessarily be good, but He is always working all things together for our good and His glory (Romans 8:28).

Going Deeper

1. In what areas of your life have you felt abandoned?

2. How has God changed you and your perspective on suffering during this season?

3. If you could post a billboard that shared a message with the world about God's character, what would that message say?

Casting all

your care

upon him,

for he careth for you.

-1 Peter 5:7 (KJV)

Chapter 2

GOD STRENGTHENS US WHEN WE'RE WEAK

Cancer, *Again?*

*O*ne Sunday morning while preaching, I noticed that I couldn't hear very well. I motioned to the person directing our sound to increase the volume on the pulpit speakers. He gave me a thumbs-up. Thinking he misunderstood me, I repeated, "Please turn it up as loud as it will go." He responded, "But, Pastor, *it is* up as loud as it will go." Puzzled, I kept preaching.

It must be a sinus infection, I thought. Both my ears were completely clogged. Soon after that Sunday morning experience, I visited the doctor, thinking it was something terribly wrong with my hearing. At that time, I was misdiagnosed. They told me it was an ear infection. It was on my third doctor's visit that the doctor told Sheila and me, to our surprise, that it looked like cancer and that we should get a second opinion and then a biopsy.

Could this be true? Four years earlier I had undergone surgery for kidney cancer; my doctor had anticipated he would soon be declaring me cancer free. But now he explained: "Nasopharyngeal carcinoma, a rare cancer found in the nasal cavity."

Tears filled our eyes. We held each other. How could cancer have crept into my nasal passage?

I needed a life jacket. So once again, I went to my Rescuer.

"God deliver me," I prayed. "What's going on?" "Help me!"

My thoughts spun. *"What does this mean? How could this be? How could this have been prevented?"*

Then, faith took root. I remembered how God had delivered me during other desperate times when I needed Him the most. He immediately brought back to mind the Scriptures that quieted my restless spirit. I recited Psalm 23 to myself with confidence. It became a personal declaration:

The Lord is my shepherd; I shall not want. He makes me lie down in green pastures; He leads me beside quiet waters. He restores my soul; He guides me in paths of righteousness for His name's sake. Even though I walk through the valley of the shadow of death, I fear no evil, for You are with me; Your rod and Your staff, they comfort me. You prepare a table before me in the presence of my enemies; You have anointed my head with oil; my cup overflows. Surely goodness and lovingkindness will follow me all the days of my life, and I will dwell in the house of the Lord forever.

Unlike the easily angered and immature seventeen-year-old E. K., I began to praise God for His goodness and greatness. I thanked Him for being a loving and kind God. I focused on Him as my compassionate Shepherd. I rejoiced because He showed me how.

NO COMPROMISE

Before I knew it, I thought less about the cancer and more about the One who could solve my problem. I wanted my faith in God, not my emotions, to guide my thinking and decision making. Here was an opportunity to live the Word that I preached. I was determined not to succumb to believing or teaching any watered-down theology.

I was determined to show God how much I trusted Him as I walked through what appeared to be the final chapter of my life. Compromise was not an option. Sure, I cried a little bit on some days . . . and a lot on other days. I prayed and prayed and prayed. I journaled my thoughts and read my Bible. I talked with trusted friends and read books and devotionals that encouraged my faith.

JESUS' SUFFERING

But the thing that helped my perspective most was I fixed my eyes on Jesus. I recalled what He did for me at Calvary. I remembered the brutality and humiliation of the cross. I remembered those first days in this shadow of death as though they happened yesterday. Aloud I said, "They pierced Him in the side for me. They nailed Him to that tree for me. He endured pain for me." It would have been so easy for Him just to come off that cross. But He chose to suffer so that I might be sanctified, justified, and redeemed.

The thought of my Savior's suffering made me reconsider my suffering. I wasn't sure what I would be up against, but I knew it could not compare to the suffering of our Lord. Suddenly I could much more easily trust God with my health problems and the fear for my future. God simply wanted me to hold on to Him as He took me farther into His Word and deeper into His will. I wasn't strong enough to do it myself but His grace was sufficient. I learned firsthand that when I was weak, He was strong.

DOES JESUS CARE?

During the first decade of the twentieth century, a man named Frank Graeff personified this truth. Popular by his nickname, Reverend Sunshine, Graeff sparkled with contagious joy. In his biography, however, he confessed to a period of deep depression. For a long, dry season, the pastor who always radiated a smile had shriveled into a bitter, critical man.

What had happened to Reverend Sunshine? He later explained that a traumatic experience had caused his personality reversal. He sulked and wallowed in self-pity. Then one day a familiar old tune began to play on the keyboard of his memory.

> *What a friend we have in Jesus,*
> *All our sins and griefs to bear!*
> *What a privilege to carry*
> *Everything to God in prayer.*[1]

The melody of the song became so sweet that he sat back and allowed it to rock him. Then those penetrating lyrics pounded at his heart. Without hesitation, Reverend Sunshine fell on his knees and repented of his sins. He confessed to carrying his heartache in his own strength— but no more. He rolled it over on his Burden-Bearer. Instead of doubting God's care, he entered into a fresh relationship with Him. He poured out his heart to God and soon experienced His joy again. He said that he felt the power of God chop away the roots and branches of bitterness that had once strangled him.

Reverend Sunshine attributed that entire process to the saving grace of God. As God nurtured him back to a spiritually healthy state of mind, the Holy Spirit brought 1 Peter 5:7 (KJV) to his remembrance, "Casting all your cares upon him; for he careth for you." That verse inspired him to write the words to the familiar song, "Does Jesus Care?" It begins with the question, "Does Jesus care when my heart is pained too deeply for mirth and song . . .?" His conclusion?

> *Oh yes, He cares. I know He cares.*
> *His heart is touched with my grief;*
> *When the days are weary; the long nights dreary,*
> *I know my Savior cares.*[2]

Does it comfort you to know Jesus cares? Invite God to chop down any roots of bitterness that have entangled your heart. Allow your brain to think it, allow your mouth to say it; ask God to help you live it with your actions. God cares.

Whatever you may be dealing with right now, God cares. He sees the pain in your body. He understands the frustration of lacking the energy that you once had. He knows all about the pressures of your job. He holds you up as you persevere in a marriage that needs revival. He knows all about those thoughts that would embarrass you to share with anyone. He sees your tears. But not only does He know what you're going through, He cares.

I have been like Reverend Sunshine before he embraced the truth. Most of us have. I live every day under the protective umbrella of 1 Peter 5:7. Yes, even pastors need encouragement. After walking with the Lord for more than fifty years, I still need the comfort of our Burden-Bearer when I consider the threat of this cancer.

CAST ALL YOUR CARES ON HIM

Perhaps you too feel weighted down by worries. If so, I would like to share with you a practical principle that can lift your spirit and remind you of God's continued concern: Cast all your cares on Him.

Does it surprise you that Christians have cares? Don't believe any watered-down theology that says Christians don't experience trials. And yes, even Christians, overwhelmed by the tidal waves of trouble, sometimes get mad at God. It is easy to blame God when you lose someone precious to you. It's easy to doubt that God loves you when the doctor delivers the news. It's even easy to wonder if God cares at all.

Jesus' disciples had a similar experience in Mark 4:35–41. Out in a boat when a great storm blew across the Sea of Galilee, they tried to control the ship with all their physical might, while Jesus slept in the back of the boat. But the storm was too great for their feeble strength, so they woke Jesus with this question: "Teacher, do You not care that we perish?"

Have you ever questioned Jesus like those disciples? *Jesus, do You not care that I'm dying?* The Word of God assures us that yes, He cares. Philippians 4:7 even says that God's peace runs guard around our hearts when difficulties, troubles, and anxieties come. When we are weak, God's strength is our protection. Whatever comes our way is not stronger than God. That's why we must cast every care upon Him.

Are you battling some debilitating disease? Perhaps you are the spouse or son/daughter of a patient who is fighting for life. Maybe you are a friend of someone with a terminal illness. Whatever your role, it is my hope that you will grasp the truth of 1 Peter 5:7 with both hands in order to be restored, renewed, and rejuvenated. Jesus cares for you. You can cast all your burdens on our great Burden-Bearer and let His joy fill your life and extricate any bitterness or anger that has strangled your heart. He cares for you.

Going Deeper

1. Name an instance when you received devastating news. What was your initial reaction? How did you deal with it after you talked to God about it?

2. Have you ever thrown a "spiritual" temper tantrum? If so, how did God speak to you during that time?

3. What Scripture, poem, or song encourages your heart when you are feeling down? How do those words minister to your need today?

NOTES

1. Joseph Scriven, "What a Friend We Have in Jesus," public domain.
2. Frank E. Graeff, "Does Jesus Care?" public domain.

I will not fail you

or forsake you. . . .

Be strong and courageous!

Do not tremble or

be dismayed,

for the Lord your God is

with you wherever you go.

—Joshua 1:5, 9

Chapter 3

GOD'S PRESENCE BRINGS PEACE IN THE STORM

Families Go Through It Too

*A*fter my diagnosis, I knew that I needed to tell my family as soon as possible—and it couldn't be over the phone. I asked them all to come over for a family meeting. I rehearsed in my mind what and how I would break the news to them. I jotted down notes as I asked God to help me to be strong.

My notes began with:

- Be sure to tell the children that God will help us to fight this together.

- Remind them that we have always stayed unified, and that's how we'll continue.

- Be open to their questions and concerns.

- Share Scripture that will encourage them.

- Tell them that my condition is in God's hand, and we are going to trust Him with our future.

It was important to me to also get the word out to people whom I could trust and people who would start praying immediately. I wanted to meet with all our church elders and deacons at one time. I planned another gathering with my mother and siblings at another time. But the children had to be first.

The hour came when all of our children gathered. I was in bed when Shenikwa entered the room. She knew the news must not be good. She climbed in the bed with me and hugged me till we cried. When we gathered in the living room, everyone held their collective breath, waiting for me to share. Cokiesha sat quietly; Emon sat up straight. The room was heavy with our somberness.

There was no other way to begin but with the news itself—cancer. Nasopharyngeal carcinoma. Prognosis: uncertain but serious. My heart's desire was that we would deal with the disease as a family.

THE QUESTIONS

They asked great questions:

"How did you get cancer?"

"Does anyone else in the family have cancer?"

"What are the treatments that are available for you?"

"Will you still be able to preach?"

"Does this cancer have anything to do with the kidney cancer from years ago?"

I answered each of those questions with no problem. Then came the question that broke my heart: "Daddy, are you afraid?"

I wanted to be the strong man who was never afraid of anyone or anything. I swallowed hard, and then tears began to roll down my face. I had to tell the truth. Sheila placed her arm around me; I looked at each of them and said, "Yes, I am afraid. I don't know what this means for us, but I do know that we have always been a family who trusted God, and we're not going to stop now."

For most of our children's lives, our daily life began around the kitchen table having morning prayer and devotions. We did that for several reasons, I told them now. First, so that they would know how to read God's Word. Next, they needed to know how to communicate with God. Most of all, they needed to know how to rely on God when we faced dark hours. That time was "our huddle," but now, it's game time. What we learned in the huddle was preparation for this.

It brought peace to my spirit to watch them dry their faces and say, "Daddy, we are here for you. We love you, and we are in this together. We are trusting God to heal you." I felt so relieved that none of them felt that God had turned His back on me. The only thing that mattered to me at that moment was their faith.

God met us in that living room that day. He provided the grace we needed in the hour we needed it. Although we each felt the grip of fear, God granted to us the courage we would need to face our fears head-on and overcome them in His strength. His presence pervaded the room and gave us peace in the storm. As Joshua reminded the children of Israel, so we lived the reality that God "will not fail you or forsake you. . . . Be strong and courageous! Do not tremble or be dismayed, for the Lord your God is with you wherever you go" (Joshua 1:5, 9).

DAY BY DAY

That day Sheila and I began to live one day at a time. Every second of the day seemed more precious. We got lost in each other's embrace. We cuddled, laughed, and "went down memory lane," sharing stories from when we first met. When our adult children entered the house, we greeted them as though we hadn't seen them in weeks. We sat longer at the dinner table; we read books together. We got a kick out of watching lighthearted movies that helped us relax and get our minds off the cancer issue.

One evening we all watched the movie *The Lion King*. After watching the father figure in the movie, Mufasa, prepare his family for their future, my children and god-children started calling me "Mufasa." God added a new spin to every part of our lives.

We began reprioritizing our calendars. Suddenly, long-scheduled meetings held no urgency for Sheila and me. Things that had once held such priority dimmed in comparison to just being together. Even our children cut down their social calendars so that we could spend more time together. We had been given a new pair of glasses that helped us see only the things that really mattered most: God, our family, and our time together.

I couldn't believe how radical the changes were. For many years I had always spent quality time with my family, but at times, I allowed the church or the nonprofit organization or the needs of members and friends to take precedence over my family's needs. As a young preacher, I often convinced myself that a good preacher is always preaching, and a good pastor is always at the church. I was so foolish!

Dinner with them was not enough. They needed my listening ear, encouragement, hugs, and guidance as the leader of our home. They needed me to be what God called me to be . . . a husband and a father. I didn't always admit it, but I needed them too. I needed their insight, their presence, their hugs, their inspiration.

As a result, I had become a better time manager, but this cancer made me even more intentional about my priorities.

Among the many adjustments that the doctor instructed us to make was the firm direction to reduce my workload. I called my assistant and asked her to clear my calendar of anything that wasn't kingdom business. I met with our assistant pastor, Bryan Carter, to discuss how to keep our church moving forward while I was out seeking treatment. With his tenacious leadership, yet humble and servant-like spirit, I was convinced that the church would be fine. Besides, this was not E. K. Bailey's church. This was *God's* church. It would be up to Him to keep things going.

MEDICAL DECISIONS

With our family and church supporting us, Sheila and I then focused on the next plan of action. At our next doctor's visit, Sheila looked at the doctor and said, "I want to see what I am fighting." I was caught off guard by her request. "I have never heard of this type of cancer, and I want to see what it looks like. Will you allow me to look to see my husband's nasal passage?" The doctor kindly complied. I was a little surprised by Sheila's request, but it encouraged me that my wife was going to take this fight seriously. At that point it seemed she had more determination to win than I did.

On many days, I woke up thinking, *Is this really happening?* We had so many unanswered questions:

- Who was the best doctor?

- How much chemotherapy and radiation would I need?

- Would this drastically change the way I lived?

- Could I still preach?

- How long is the recuperation time? Will this cancer spread?

I couldn't stop thinking about the what-ifs. I really wanted the Lord to show us what the next step would be so that our hearts could be eased.

My doctor scheduled a second opinion for me. After it had been confirmed that I did indeed have cancer, we were told that I would have several weeks of chemo and radiation. We had friends, including hospital administrators, doctors, and nurses, ask us to consider the world-renowned M. D. Anderson Cancer Center in Houston as our treatment center.

The more we read and researched and prayed about it, the more we settled on M. D. Anderson. Only one problem loomed in our minds—would my insurance cover it? We filled out a lot of paperwork and waited for a response from our insurance company. We really wanted them to just call us to tell us the answer, but policies had to take precedence. So we waited.

IN GOD'S WAITING ROOM

Some friends, out of their concern for me, pressed us to get treatment right away. Instead, I felt that God wanted me to wait and trust Him. I knew His answer was yes, so I didn't pace or fret. We checked the mail daily and waited some more. To some it may not have been a logical step, but we were certain that God had charge of the timing and He wanted us to wait on Him.

What wonderful things God does in His children when they are forced to wait! Sitting in God's waiting room is never fun or comfortable, but it's where the child of God learns the most about the character of God and the depth of their faith. Contrary to popular opinion, experience is not the best teacher, but it is the most painful one. In the storm of those early days of decision, God gave me His peace. In those long hours of waiting, I was comforted by the truth that God loved me. Despite life's discomfort and pain, He loved me and cared for my needs. Read of His concern for you and for me in Psalm 103:1–5:

> *Bless the Lord, O my soul,*
> *And all that is within me, bless His holy name.*
> *Bless the Lord, O my soul,*
> *And forget none of His benefits;*
> *Who pardons all your iniquities, . . .*
> *Who crowns you with lovingkindness and compassion;*
> *Who satisfies your years with good things.*

HOPE IN GOD'S WORD

His Word also gives perspective of how we handle this road of affliction. One of my favorite verses is, "We are afflicted in every way, but not crushed; perplexed, but not despairing; persecuted, but not forsaken; struck down, but not destroyed" (2 Corinthians 4:8–9).

When our health is transitioning, doesn't God's Word bring us hope for our hearts—hope to know that we are not forsaken?

We must also be careful not to think that Christians are supposed to have perfect lives that do not include illness or suffering. Not only that, we must understand that God may not reveal to us why He has allowed us to become sick. Some things will remain a mystery. While some of your questions will be addressed in the Bible, some will not. At such times, we are forced to walk by faith, trusting the Lord to show us the next step as it is needed. We must, however, keep our eyes on Jesus.

Do not succumb to watered-down theology on your journey through your illness. The Bible promises that you have a secure destiny, not a downhill slide once you've invited Christ to come into your life. Bible instruction alone will not result in instant solutions to problems. We are called to walk by faith.

TIME WITH GOD

In order to gain intimacy with God during your illness, you must spend time with Him. Rise early in the morning, and talk with the Lord, read your Bible, and sit quietly in His presence. Just as you can recall falling in love with a special person by getting to know him or her and by spending time together, God desires that we would fall in love with Him. He will give you insight on how to handle your affliction. He will cradle you in His arms when you are uncomfortable and confused. He will fill your heart with joy as you bask in His presence, and He will reveal to you more about His multifaceted personality as you learn about His ways.

Rely on the Bible as a blueprint for daily living as you learn how to walk in obedience and trust Him daily.

When people become sick, they often wallow in self-pity. I know firsthand what it feels like to do both, but God has called us to rise above our present situation and to follow the map He gives us in His Word. Second Timothy 3:16 (KJV) says, "All Scripture is given by inspiration of God, and is profitable for doctrine, for reproof, for correction, for instruction in righteousness."

During the time of illness and recuperation, as you wait on the Lord, allow Him to renew your mind, to refresh your spirit, and to teach you how to present your bodies to Him.

"Therefore I urge you, [brothers and sisters], by the mercies of God, to present your bodies a living and holy sacrifice, acceptable to God, which is your spiritual service of worship. And do not be conformed to this world, but be transformed by the renewing of your mind, so that you may prove what the will of God is, that which is good and acceptable and perfect" (Romans 12:1–2).

Going Deeper

1. If you were told you had a terminal illness, would you share it with your family? Why or why not?

2. What decisions do you need to make about your immediate future? Your long-term future?

3. What would you do differently if you were told that you only had one year to live?

Now may the God of hope

fill you with

all joy and peace

in believing,

so that you will abound

in hope by the power

of the Holy Spirit.

–Romans 15:13

Chapter 4

GOD'S SOVEREIGNTY IS OUR SECURITY

A Leap of Faith to Houston

The day finally arrived that we received the "highly anticipated letter." Hanging on its every word, we read it slowly and carefully: "Rev. E. K. Bailey, your request has been denied."

"How could this be?" I was puzzled and hurt. Sheila and I sat in silence. I was sure the Lord had given me peace about this. "I know what this paper says, Sheila, but God told me that He was going to work it out."

"So, what should we do?" she asked.

"We're going to make plans as though the answer were yes."

I have said to my congregation time and time again, "Faith is acting like something is so, even when it is not so, so that it will be so." Praise God! This was a great way for us to live out what we believed.

When Sheila said "Okay" and started packing our things for our move to Houston, I was so glad for this woman God had given me as my partner. She could have said, "But, baby, the letter says you cannot be covered." Instead she joined me in trusting God with what seemed impossible. God gave us peace to move ahead, trusting Him for each step.

We forged ahead and shared with our family that we believed that my treatment would come from this reputable hospital in Houston. We told them that we would probably have to move for a month or two. We even were honest with them about the fact that our insurance company turned down my request to be covered but that we were clearly trusting God with this one. They were excited about our leap of faith, and that helped us even more to move forward on our decision.

PRAYING, TAKING ACTION, AND PRAYING

We called our prayer teams at church, our church leaders, close friends, and other family members and asked them to pray for us and with us. Several people started making calls to state representatives, council members, and other influential people who could help us overturn this decision. We even pleaded with several doctors to see if their influence could help get us a new decision. Edna Pemberton, a member of our church, who has always "had my back," even called the White House. To her surprise, she said that the person who answered the phone said, "Oh, I know your pastor. We will be praying for him, and we'll see what we can do."

We kept praying and working. A few minutes later, my doctor called me and said, "E.K., I really don't think this will be overturned. The company never changes its mind in a case like this. Your treatment will be over $100,000." I told the family that we were going to keep praying and packing. Finally, it was time to head out.

My buddy Hansel Cunningham and brother-in-law Rick Jordan assured me that they would travel with Sheila and me to help out in any way. My longtime friend, Melba Smith, offered his Winnebago—the same vehicle that moved one of my daughters to college was now going to move me to Houston.

DOCTOR ON THE LINE

As we sat in the living room on the day we were making this leap of faith, we were hugging and going over last-minute duties and details. Then the phone rang. Everyone was still and quiet.

Like a scene in a movie, we all stopped in our tracks, wondering whether there was a twist in our "unpredictable plot." It was my doctor on the line.

"I don't know how this happened," he began. "The insurance company reversed their decision."

I had to sit down and catch my breath because I couldn't believe what I was hearing. My heart leapt for joy. God was turning our midnight into morning right before our very eyes. We cried; we thanked God. I told my family and friends to write down in a journal what they witnessed. I wanted them to remember how God provided for us on this day and how He answered our prayers.

HOUSTON, HERE WE COME

Next, we jumped into the Winnebago and headed down Highway 45 to Houston. No need to wait—we were packed, ready to go! It felt good to ride, laugh, and pray with Rick, Melba, Hansel, and Sheila. They always seemed to be among my most consistent encouragers.

So many emotions flooded my heart. I was thankful to have an opportunity to receive care from one of the most prestigious hospitals in the country. I was so joyful that the Lord had opened the door for our insurance company to cover it. On the other hand, I already sensed the distinct feeling of homesickness. I was accustomed to traveling but had always been home in a few days. This time, we were talking a month, maybe two.

As we got closer to Houston, I wrestled with the fear of the unknown. How would chemotherapy change me? Would I become much darker? Frail? Bald? I dreaded what radiation and chemotherapy would do to me. I also can't stand being in close quarters and feared tests that would put me in a tube. Isn't it something to think about— the very thing that will potentially change or disfigure us is the same thing that will save our lives. I didn't know what to expect, but I wanted to trust the Lord with my fears. I resolved there was no good in getting worked up over the "what-ifs." Everything was in the Lord's hands.

We reached Houston and entered the M. D. Anderson Rotary House. It was so nice; our rooms were like a small apartment—including a stove, refrigerator, and a television —and handicap accessible. It was much smaller than our home, but it was certainly enough space for us to make it a home away from home.

OUR HOME AWAY FROM HOME

Sheila and I felt at home immediately. Each room was complete with a living area, a bathroom, and a kitchen. It had a beautiful view of the city and felt very cozy. I could see why they were always sold out. Everyone, the staff as well as patients, had made it a community where people genuinely cared for one another. Many of the guests checked on one another after radiation and chemotherapy, and some even exchanged "thinking of you" gifts. If one person had a bad day, then others were seen praying for them or sending notes to their rooms to encourage them. I could tell that it was going to be a place where we could have friends and fun (if my strength would allow it) and time alone to deal with the illness and the effects of the treatments.

M. D. Anderson is enormous, a city within walls. As we toured the facilities, I looked around in awe. Staff members smiled at us and asked us our hometown. I was impressed when I came upon the hospital's mission, vision, and core values. I have shared with leaders the importance of having a church mission, mission statement, and even a personal life mission statement. To me, establishing one always helps us to remain committed to what matters most, God's agenda for our lives. To notice that the hospital had done the same thing made me feel that they were very intentional about providing quality care with a spirit of excellence.

As we walked around "this city," I witnessed their commitment to their vision. Anderson's vision is this: "We shall be the premier cancer center in the world, based on the excellence of our people, our research-driven patient care and our science. We are making cancer history."

In every corner of the hospital, there was something on the walls or on a desk or on a sign that reminded us of God's presence. My mind and my body relaxed as the Lord confirmed that I was supposed to be there at that time.

It was clear that God was walking with us. His presence was so sweet. He was certainly making us feel welcome in our new home and confident in Him as we anticipated the days ahead.

Going Deeper

1. What was your last big faith step? What did others say about your decision? Have you ever experienced God turning your midnight into morning?

2. Do you have the faith to trust God when your future is uncertain?

3. List three things about God's track record in your life that shows Him to be trustworthy.

Do not fear, for I am with you;

do not anxiously look about you,

for I am your God.

I will strengthen you,

surely I will help you,

surely I will uphold you

with My righteous right hand.

—*Isaiah 41:10*

Chapter 5

THE POWER OF GOD WILL FIGHT FOR ME

Facing an Unknown Future

*E*xhausted from our full tour of the hospital, I took a nap when we got back to our new home-away-from-home and then spent some time in prayer to get ready for my first visit with the doctors. I journaled about our visit and even started writing notes for upcoming sermons. I may not have been able to preach in the Concord pulpit for a while, but I was still a preacher. I wanted to chronicle the lessons that I had learned up until this point and was excited about the lessons that were still yet to come in this healing journey.

Houston seemed to burst at the seams with members of the Bailey family and our extended family and longtime friends. My first cousin, Don Bailey, assistant at another hospital, offered his help to us every day after he got off work.

Familiar with the journey we were beginning, Don knew that I would see some difficult days and that traveling back and forth from the Rotary House to the hospital would at times be challenging. He would provide a wheelchair on the days that I didn't feel up to the walk. Don was an excellent caregiver and a loving family member. We were humbled by his kindness.

The committed pastors and wives in Houston showered Sheila and me with love. Little did we know that the days ahead would become dark sometimes, and their prayers, cards, visits, and even their availability to run errands would help us keep going.

Throughout our treatment time, they brought food to us, prayed with us, even arranged haircuts for me and assisted Sheila with trips to the grocery store. Others brought us encouraging books to read and snacks. My niece Pam made regular Monday visits, and her hearty laughter and sweet spirit kept our spirits high. My cousin Rosa Pearl and other caring family members came often too. It was wonderful to feel so much love.

LEARNING ABOUT CANCER

Sheila and I began the morning with the Lord, ate breakfast, and strolled from our room across the breezeway to the hospital. Besides a few jitters, I felt calm. To my surprise, we met people who heard that we were coming and told us that they had been praying for us. We met with several doctors, all of whom were compassionate and understanding. They didn't rush us or ignore our questions.

The first thing that we needed to understand was the cancer that we were fighting. Cancer of any kind, they said, develops when cells grow out of control. Normal body cells grow, divide, and die in an orderly fashion. Cells in most parts of the body divide only to replace worn-out or dying cells and to repair injuries. Cancer cells, however, continue to grow and divide. They outlive normal cells and continue to form new abnormal cells. Cancer cells initially develop because of damage to DNA.

We also wanted to understand more about the particular type of cancer that I have. We knew that it was found in the nasal passage, and that it is rare. Nasopharyngeal cancer develops in the nasopharynx, a one-inch, boxlike chamber toward the base of the skull. The cancer tends to spread widely, is not often treated by surgery, and has different risk factors from most other oral cancers. Each layer of tissue in the nasopharynx contains several types of cells. Different cancer cells can develop within each cell. Tumors, both benign and malignant, can penetrate into surrounding tissues and spread to other parts of the body.

The doctors explained that there are no known risk factors to this cancer, which means that it could not have been prevented. It felt good to know that I didn't bring this on myself.

GETTING READY FOR THE FIRST DAY OF TREATMENT

The doctors then confirmed what the Dallas doctors had said. I needed to be willing to be in their care for at least a month and a half to undergo radiation and chemotherapy. They showed me a "mask of assimilation" that they would make for me. First, I would put on the mask of my upper body and I would lay down on a rotating table. As the tabled turned, red lasers would penetrate the mask and "zap" the area where the cancer was growing in my nasal passage.

Suddenly this wasn't a "cakewalk" anymore. I wanted to get well, but I didn't want to be enclosed in that mask. I surely didn't want to get up on that cold table with the mask on my face. And the idea of the red lasers "zapping me" made me even more uneasy.

There was no use pretending. I just couldn't see myself in any test or procedure that ignited my claustrophobia. It was an area that I needed to seek the Lord in every moment. I remember getting in another piece of equipment for an MRI at another doctor's office at another time. My friend Hansel encouraged me; he even got into the machine to show me how easy it was. I laughed and told him that it just wasn't that easy for me. He cheered for me and prayed for me, but I was still afraid. Needless to say, the Lord helped me out in that situation years ago. He reminded me of Scriptures and songs that soothed me as I tested.

Now here I was at M. D. Anderson, faced with a similar test. I focused on how God had helped me before. One saving grace was I could listen to my favorite CDs while in the tube. Thank God, when I began the procedures, the music helped me unwind. Ralph Waldo Emerson once said, "Do the thing that you fear, and the death of fear is certain." I, therefore, confronted my fears and invited the Lord into my treatments. I leaned hard on His presence to get me through each session.

I used to look at the people passing by me in the hospital with such compassion. Their skin was darkening and their hair had fallen out. Now I was that patient people looked on with compassion. Sometimes I didn't even recognize myself in the mirror. I journaled about how awful I felt and how I battled depression creeping in on the days I felt the worst. At first I felt like a trooper, but some days, I felt like an injured athlete on the sideline. Some days I prayed and asked God to give me the strength to endure, while on other days all I could do was moan.

FAMILY PEP RALLIES

Sheila was in every way my helpmeet. She read me Scripture and placed encouraging notes around the room, "You can do it! . . . Stick with it! . . . You're great! . . . Superb job!" That helped me muster up a smile. Shenikwa made a calendar to show the number of days that I had been there and the days that led up to my completion of the treatments. As the days passed, my enthusiasm grew as I saw the last date approaching.

Cokiesha visited every few weeks, and on one of her visits she arranged for the family to have a mock Olympic ceremony in order to encourage me. Each of them presented me with a medal and shared with me how much they loved me and how they saw me going for the gold. I was speechless as they affirmed me. If their intention was to make me feel like a champion, they truly succeeded.

As a pastor I had encouraged people for almost thirty years, but now, in my moment of need, the Lord allowed others to replenish my spirit and to lift my head. My family and I began to understand a language that could not be put into words. Some days I could talk and smile, and some days I couldn't. They began to understand what I wanted to say with my eyes and by expressions on my face and even by holding my hand. The treatments had severely changed the way I looked and felt, but they always made me feel like I was the same strong leader and provider for our home.

But more important than that, the Lord showed me that He would fight for me more than my family, my doctor, and I ever could. He assured me that He would help me to face my unknown future.

GOD WILL FIGHT FOR ME

God began to whisper so many things in my ear that reminded me of His ability to fight for me. He brought specific instances in His Word to mind where He fought for others. I had to come to grips with the reality that my future was unknown, but also that my Savior, my Healer, My Redeemer was not unknown. In Psalm 46, I read about the victory over fear of an uncertain future.

> *God is our refuge and strength, a very present help in trouble. Therefore we will not fear, though the earth should change and though the mountains slip into the heart of the sea; though its waters roar and foam, though the mountains quake at its swelling pride.*
>
> *There is a river whose streams make glad the city of God, the holy dwelling places of the Most High. God is in the midst of her, she will not be moved; God will help her when morning dawns. The nations made an uproar, the kingdoms tottered; He raised His voice, the earth melted. The Lord of hosts is with us; the God of Jacob is our stronghold.*
>
> *Come, behold the works of the Lord. . . . "Cease striving and know that I am God; I will be exalted among the nations, I will be exalted in the earth." The Lord of hosts is with us; the God of Jacob is our stronghold.*

I invite you to look with me at a scenic film in 2 Kings 19 that played in my mind as I recalled the miraculous power of God:

GOD WILL FIGHT FOR US

The scene is Jerusalem. The dreaded Assyrian army had marched down from the north, and now the mighty army has deployed themselves around the city of God. The watchers on Jerusalem's wall see the flag of the Assyrian Empire blowing in the wind. They see the battering rams, the slings, the boulders, even the scaling ladders that will be used in the battle.

At first Hezekiah, the king of Jerusalem, hopes to appease Sennacherib, the leader of the Assyrian army, by paying an enormous tribute. But Sennacherib knows he needs to conquer Jerusalem or else there will be nothing but trouble in the future. Encouraged by the prophetic preaching of Isaiah, King Hezekiah refuses to give in to Sennacherib's taunting. God will fight for Jerusalem.

Sennacherib sends word to Hezekiah, "Surrender or accept the consequences." In spite of the uncertain future, Hezekiah holds on to his faith. The time for talking is over. All negotiations are off. Now they are ready to do battle.

It is getting toward evening, so the Assyrian army decides to get a good night's rest before cranking up the engines of war the next day. Tomorrow they will have success over Jerusalem! The soldiers bed down. The guards watch from their posts. The generals sleep in their tents. The officers pore over last-minute strategies.

AN ANGEL IN THE MIDST

Second Kings 19:35 reports that God dismissed an angel that night. As the old preacher would say, "That angel left the coast of Glory quicker than right now and sooner than at once." And like the night east wind, he blew through the Assyrian camp. By the time he got back to heaven at the break of dawn, 185,000 soldiers lay dead around the walls of Jerusalem. That is the way it was.

"When [the] men [of Israel] rose early in the morning, behold, all [the enemy soldiers] were dead" (verse 35). Imagine the delirious delight that daybreak brought to the streets of Jerusalem. The watchers on the wall knew something drastic had taken place overnight. At daybreak, there was no blowing of the bugles. No sounding of the trumpets. No rallying of the troops. There was only silence echoing from the enemy camp. Buzzards swirled over the Assyrians. The engines of war had been shut down.

Then the spies came back with the word that all of the Assyrian soldiers were dead. Nothing but corpses now lay around the walls of Jerusalem, and the people in Jerusalem began to sing praises to God. Their dreaded enemy, Sennacherib, had been soundly defeated.

When God got through with that uncertain situation, the Assyrians, who had expected to have victory, experienced defeat. The people of God, who had expected to be overcome, experienced victory. God protected, preserved, and rescued His people from an impossible situation, and I am trusting Him to do the same with me.

God works behind the scenes on our behalf. I am certain of one thing, and I encourage you to be certain of this as well. You can look ahead to the future, not because you have the best physicians, not because you have secured your will, not even because you have money, a loving family, and caring friends. You can look ahead with certainty because *the Lord of hosts is with you.*

Going Deeper

1. Is there a film that you can replay in your mind of God's miraculous power?

2. When was the last time you needed God to fight for you? Describe how He did it.

Pray

without ceasing.

–1 Thessalonians 5:17

Chapter 6

GOD DELIGHTS IN US WHEN WE PRAY

Enrolled in the School of Prayer

A few years ago a dear friend and colleague, Warren Wiersbe, preached a message at our Expository Preaching Conference. His words resonated with my heart. Let me share with you how God spoke to me.

*I*n every level of schooling, I've seen God's hand directing my maturity, but as much as I have learned in my formal classes, I've learned even more just going through the process of growing up in the Lord. Through challenges and relationships, God has made me a man who would desire spiritual, moral, and academic excellence.

In the same way that school shapes us, prayer shapes us more. It causes us to desire personal, spiritual, and moral excellence. It enhances the way we think and live. Through prayer we become better spouses, better children, better employers and employees, and better stewards of our time. Most of all, we become better representatives of the kingdom of God. Just as our teachers used lessons, homework, and encouragement to maximize our academic potential, God uses prayer to stretch our faith muscles and to maximize our spiritual potential. Prayer enhances everything about us.

Our lives fall short of what God desires for us if we neglect the opportunity to attend the "school of prayer." In this chapter I invite you to visit the school of prayer with me.

PRAYER SHOULD BE LIKE BREATHING

Throughout my illness, I have found myself constantly on my knees, talking to God. When I can't kneel to pray, I sit or lie with my eyes closed and my heart in a posture of reverence. Even when I am weak, I am certain that God is still strong, mighty, and at work in my life. Prayer gives me a full tank when my confidence, courage, and strength are running on empty.

So real is my dependence on God that prayer has become as regular as breathing. It helps me greet each new day and allows me to wrap up my nights. I have learned that prayer governs our faith walk as believers. It governs our belief system, our attitude about our circumstances, and our health challenges, our suffering and setbacks.

There are three legitimate ways to get what you want in life—by thinking, working, and most of all, by praying.

Most of us pride ourselves on being good thinkers. We boast at how hard we work on our jobs. But if we are honest, we admit that we do not take enough time to pray. Prayer becomes our escape hatch when something we do doesn't go right or when we are zapped of our mental and physical energy. Most people would rather work than pray. But we are at our best when we pray.

Prayer is mysterious. When we pray, we are in touch with three worlds at the same time. Nothing else in life allows this. When we pray, our prayer (1) goes up to God in worship, (2) out to man in work and witness, and (3) down to Satan in warfare. So, if we want to worship, work, witness, and war, we need to go to God in prayer.

"TEACH US TO PRAY"

Jesus taught His disciples many things, but they *asked* Him to teach only one thing: "Lord, teach us to pray" (Luke 11:1). They recognized the mystery. They knew that if they learned to pray, "all these [other] things" would be added unto them (see Matthew 6:33).

If we could have overheard the conversation among the disciples about Jesus and prayer, how would it have sounded? Imagine them trailing behind the Teacher. Maybe they said, "You know, we have seen many rabbis in our time, but He is different than all the rest."

"Do you think it's in His clothes?" one disciple may have asked.

"It could be," another may have answered. "You know, the other day that woman elbowed her way through the crowd until she was able to touch the hem of His garment."

"I don't think it's His clothes, because we wear the same kind He wears," still another would have remarked. "It's not His diet either 'cause we eat the same stuff."

"No, it's how Jesus prays," a fourth disciple would have concluded.

Then they approached the Lord. "Rabbi, we've been watching You pray for years. We have been taught in our rituals and ceremonies how to pray, and we pronounce our prayers with eloquence, but You have power with Your praying. Lord, will You teach us to pray like You pray?"

They had walked with Jesus, they ate with Jesus, sat with Jesus, and had prayed all of their lives, but they never understood the power in prayer. Maybe for the first time in their lives, they discovered that prayer for them had been a form, but for Jesus, prayer was a force. They, too, wanted to experience the power of prayer that Jesus experienced. They saw Him go into prayer sad and sorrowful, but they saw Him come out of prayer singing and shouting. They saw Him go into prayer despondent, but they saw Him come out of prayer delivered. They saw Him go into prayer crawling like a caterpillar, but they saw Him come out of prayer flying.

"Teach us to pray, Lord."

I imagine the Lord said to them, "Since you want to be taught, let's go to class."

THE FIRST THREE LEVELS OF PRAYER

During the trying seasons of illness, we have a special opportunity to learn from Jesus' example. *Jesus first takes us through grade-school praying. Grade-school praying teaches us to grasp the necessity of prayer.*

You cannot live the Christian life without prayer. I don't care how long you have been saved; you have to allow Jesus to live through you. None of us can live the Christian life in our own strength. If you don't pray, you can't resist the temptations that will come your way.

Through prayer you release God to live His life through you.

We can't learn from the life of Christ without looking at His prayer life. In the gospel of Luke alone, we find nine references alone to Jesus praying or urging others to pray (5:16; 6:12; 6:28; 9:28; 11:1; 18:1; 22:40; 22:41; 22:46). Jesus was the second person of the Trinity. Yet, He prayed.

He was conceived by the Holy Spirit; yet, He prayed. He lived a completely sinless life; yet, He prayed. He was always obedient to the Father; yet, He prayed. If Jesus had to pray, how much more must we? Without prayer, it's easy for us to curse God when cancer and other diseases enter our bodies.

Prayer flies in the face of human nature. Prayer flies in the face of human logic, because we think that we can either think our way, manipulate our way, or pay our way out of everything. Often we think we can control our way, like Jonah tried to do. If Jonah could speak now, I'm sure he'd tell us, "You can't think your way out. You can't talk your way out. You have to pray your way out."

Grade-school prayer is important, but don't stop there. *Graduate to high-school prayer. High-school praying teaches us that we have to pray in God's will.*

Recall when you first began to pray. Do you remember not knowing what to pray for? It just seemed exciting to talk to God, didn't it? You just talked to God and prayed all over the place. It seemed like God just followed you around, blessed your prayers, and answered your prayers. Then, you prayed and nothing happened.

You felt confused. *Why is God ignoring me?* But He wasn't —He was just advancing you from grade-school praying to high-school praying. In grade school, you prayed all over the place, and God blessed it to encourage you to keep it up. But, now that you're in high school, He says that you have to pray according to His will. Stop asking the Lord to bless what you're doing; now ask the Lord to help you do what He blesses.

Have you noticed that young children will ask for anything? They don't know the danger of what they are asking for. A nine-year-old will ask for a diet of ice cream and candy because he doesn't know the danger of an unbalanced diet. When we are young in the Lord, we will ask for anything. But as we grow, we ask for what the Father wants to give.

In high school, you don't just pray for what you want; you pray for what the Father wants to give. Do you want to know what God blesses so that you can get in on it? He blesses His Word. He blesses His way, and He blesses His will. When the Holy Spirit delivers your prayer to the throne of God, the first thing God looks for is the signature of His Son. If it has His signature, it is in His will, and it is in His authority.

Don't stop at high-school praying. *Move on to college-praying, which is learning the secret of answered prayer.* The disciples did not say, "Lord, teach us how to pray." They said, "Lord, teach us to pray." The difference lies in how to do something and actually doing it. Because Jesus knows the desires of our hearts, He answered both in His model prayer that begins in Matthew 6:9, known as the "Lord's Prayer."

First of all, as we begin to pray, we should praise and adore. Don't rush into God's presence and start telling Him what you want. Praise Him first because of who He is. Praise Him for His majesty. Praise Him for His sovereignty. Praise Him for His creative genius. Praise Him for His splendor, and praise Him because of who He was yesterday, is today, and will be tomorrow.

Go from adoration to thanksgiving. Before asking for anything, thank Him for what He has done for you and your family. Thank Him for His faithfulness. Thank Him for His goodness, His grace, and His greatness. After you spend time in thanksgiving, transition to intercession.

Thank God for other people. Do you know lost people who need your prayers? We ought to pray that God would touch our society. We ought to pray that God would help church members to be unified and neighbors to be friendly and family members to get along. We ought to be excited about praying for other people—people all over the world and people right down the street.

As we continue in prayer, make your personal petitions. Our foreparents used to sing a song that said, "Call Him up and tell Him what you want." Have you shared with the Lord what is on your heart? Did you tell Him what you need? First Thessalonians 5:17 says, "Pray without ceasing." Praying without ceasing does not mean a continuous articulation of human words but a steady posture of your heart. When you are in tune with God, you know when God is talking to you and you are living a life that is obedient to His will.

True prayer reflects your relationship with your Father. I recall when my son, Emon, turned sixteen. I asked him how he wanted to celebrate this special milestone. He asked me to cook his favorite meal, take him swimming, and let lots of friends come to the home to celebrate. And then, "I want you to take all of us to that entertainment center with race cars, at your expense."

I said okay to each of these requests. Then he added, "Daddy, on Sunday morning, we want to get up and go to church." Finally he said, "I want to close out my birthday by going to my favorite restaurant, the Barbecue Pit—your treat." I agreed to all of those things with no problem because my son was turning sixteen.

Because he is my son, he got to enjoy the gifts and the fellowship that surrounded his birthday. Because he is my son, he had a permanent room in my house. Because he is my son, there was always food on the table for him. Because he is my son, I bought his clothes, I paid for his education. He got all of that just because he bears my name, because he bears my image. He is my son.

Now there is more he could get, but he couldn't get it just because he is my son. He got it only if he acted like my son. If he acted like my son, he got my money. If he acted like my son, he could drive my car. If he acted like my

Four Levels of Prayer

1. **Grade-school Prayer.** *These prayers recognize we must pray; we must pray to resist the temptations that we will face and to invite God to live His life through you. Even Jesus began here, knowing His power came through prayer.*

2. **High-school Prayer.** *These prayers seek to know God's will and then ask God to help us follow it. We want to pray according to His will. Instead of asking the Lord to bless what you're doing, you now ask the Lord to help you do what He blesses.*

3. **College Prayer.** *These prayers focus on God by praising Him for who He is and thanking Him for what He does and for the people He uses in our lives. Such prayers precede intercession for others and ourselves. In fact praise and thanksgiving lead naturally for caring about the needs of others.*

4. **Graduate-level Prayer.** *These prayers seek God's best for others and ourselves. They go beyond material needs and good health to what is best. This includes the Holy Spirit filling and controlling our lives and the deeper inner qualities like holiness, virtue, and mercy.*

son, he could get tickets to the show. If he acted like my son, there was so much more for him.

It is the same thing with our Father. You get a lot because you belong to Him, but if you act like His child, if you talk like His child, if you walk like His child, He'll bless you. God doesn't bless you out of obligation or out of force; God blesses you out of love.

Do you know why the Lord blesses you and delivers you out of a Red Sea situation? It is because when He delivers you, He wants you to praise Him. When you praise Him, He will deliver you next out of a lions' den. When you praise Him, He will deliver you out of a fiery furnace. Why? So you can praise Him. You can go around, not bragging about what you did, but you tell everybody what *God* did.

THE FOURTH LEVEL OF PRAYER

We have talked about various levels of prayer, starting with grade school. In grade school, you learn that you have to walk with the Lord in order to pray. High school teaches that you have to pray right. College teaches you the secret of prayer: to stay in constant communion with God. Now, we come to the graduate level of prayer. Few people matriculate to this level.

The graduate level of praying is to learn to pray for God's best.

Jesus says, "If you then, being evil, know how to give good gifts to your children, how much more will your Father who is in heaven give what is good to those who ask Him!" (Matthew 7:11).

The Holy Spirit represents the best that God has to offer. From the point that you are saved, you never again have to pray for the Holy Spirit. All of the Holy Spirit you will ever get comes in at the time of salvation. Of course, you can be indwelt by the Holy Spirit but not controlled by the Holy Spirit. The Holy Spirit is what Ephesians 5:18 talks about. "And do not get drunk with wine, . . . but be filled with the Spirit." That means that the Holy Spirit is controlling your life. To be filled with the Spirit is not about how much of the Spirit you have but how much of you the Spirit has.

Too much of our praying centers on material things. Now there is nothing wrong with asking God to meet your physical needs. The apostle Paul said, "My God will supply all your needs" (Philippians 4:19). He's your Father and He delights in providing what you need. Our trouble is praying for things that we'd like rather than what we need.

Therefore,

> It is all right to ask for food, but it is better to ask for faith.

It is all right to ask for money, but it is better to ask for mercy.

It is all right to ask for cash, but it is better to ask for character.

It is all right to pray for a house, but it is better to pray for holiness.

It is all right to pray for a relationship, but it is better to pray for righteousness.

It is all right to pray for a promotion, but it is better to pray for power.

If I have power, the world will know that I have been with the Lord.

If I have power, the world will know that His anointing is on my head.

It is all right to know botany, but it is better to know the Lily of the Valley and the Rose of Sharon.

It is all right to have diamonds, but it is better to have the pearl of great value (Matthew 13:46).

It's all right to have your name written down in many books, but it's better to have your name written down in the Lamb's Book of Life.

It's all right to live in a fine mansion, but it's better to have a building that is not made with hands (2 Corinthians 5:1).

If you know the Lord, you ought to talk with Him. He is longing to hear from you.

Going Deeper

1. If you could ask God for anything, what would it be?

2. How old were you when prayer became a priority? Who taught you how to pray? How does their prayer life inspire you?

3. Are you intentional about having a special time each day to spend with God in prayer, or do you do it whenever time permits? How do you gauge the amount of time you spend with the Lord each day?

Write out a prayer below. It can be a couple of sentences or a few paragraphs. Write what flows from your heart to the Lord's heart. Imagine that your words were a love note and tell the Lord why you adore Him. Share with the Lord what concerns you the most. Finally, tell Him how much you trust Him with your burdens.

Faith is

the assurance of

things hoped for,

the conviction of

things not seen.

–Hebrews 11:1

Chapter 7

GOD IS PRESENT IN THE DARK

Turning on God's Night Scope

As the weeks rolled by, I had become accustomed to the days and times of chemo and radiation. I had even grown comfortable wearing the mask. My eyes were fixed on the bright calendar that Sheila had hung in our room. At the end of every day, she'd mark through the date so that I could see how many days I had left in treatment. I felt like a kid counting down the days until summer vacation.

I had become homesick. I missed my own bed. I missed my favorite pillow. I missed the familiar scent of our home. I missed our loving church members. I missed our pets, Pretty (our cat) and D.T. (our dog). I missed standing on the porch and yelling to neighbors Lloyd and Tressie Blue to come over. I missed opening the door and yelling out

Lloyd's name, "B-L-U-E" until his door opened and he waved.

MISSING THE ACTION

I missed our family's late Sunday-night talks while sitting around eating hot wings and watching TV. And I missed those Sunday afternoons, when my children, along with my goddaughters, Yomica, Tan, and Alicia, came over after worship service to be with Sheila and me. After everyone had dinner and a nap or two, we'd gather together and chat and laugh.

I missed everything familiar about living in Dallas. I missed lunch with local pastors and young preachers. I missed our prayer service and working in my office. I missed staff meetings where we had a good time singing, praying, and learning biblical principles that assisted us in serving our church more effectively. I missed leadership and elders' meetings.

I missed my barber, seeing friends at the gym, and reclining in my favorite green La-Z-Boy chair.

I missed Jermaine Concord Johnson, whose mother named him after our church. He is one of my favorite young members who has special needs. He always greeted me with a bear hug or a high five as he burst into the church's lounge each week shouting, "H-e-y, Pastor Bailey!"

We appreciated everyone's kindness in Houston, but the old adage rings true: "There is no place like home."

UNDER THE WEIGHT OF WEAKNESS

On top of feeling homesick, I felt fatigue, woozy, and irritable a lot. Sometimes I didn't recognize my own face in the mirror. My eyes were bright and wide, and my skin was much darker. I had lost weight as the radiation made my throat raw. I no longer could swallow, so I had to eat through a feeding tube. The smell of the milklike substance that ran through the tube made me nauseous. And every morning I noticed more hair that had shed on my pillow.

All of my life I had been a confident and optimistic fellow. But as my health changed and my physical strength weakened, I felt depression creeping in.

As friends and family dropped by, I could tell that many of them were surprised to see my change in appearance. They were kind and gracious, but I knew that some were uncomfortable and others were heartbroken for me.

Every visitor, however, made an effort to say things that were encouraging and uplifting. Some chose to stay quiet and to minister to us with their presence. Others, however well intended, blurted out the wrong words at the wrong time. If I have learned anything through this journey, it is to pray before I say anything to anyone, especially if the person is suffering and hurting.

My diabetes was closely monitored as the combination of treatments prevented me from having complete feeling in my hands and legs. Cold was difficult to tolerate after the treatment began. I always needed blankets around me and sometimes gloves on my hands. When I did walk, I had to lean on a cane or a walker.

I was definitely living life differently now. I felt like I was living each day in the dark. I had to learn how to maneuver in this newfound, uninvited darkness as I leaned on God to be my guide and my stability.

USING GOD'S NIGHTSCOPE

Who hasn't gotten up in the middle of the night and headed for the bathroom or dashed for the phone and run smack-dab into a wall or a bedpost? Does your situation feel dark right now? Do you feel the pain of stumbling around in your illness? Do you need God's help in your "midnight situations"?

During World War II, scientists developed a technology that enabled the soldiers to be more efficient in their night fighting. The technology was applied to a sniperscope that allows the soldier to see in the dark. What a great advantage over the enemy!

The soldier wears the sniperscope like goggles. The scope sends out an invisible, intangible, infrared ray and reflects back visual images of whatever objects are in their path. The soldier therefore "sees" without light.

❖ ❖ ❖

Comfort in the Night

We are to seek God's comfort during the nights of our lives. God will bestow comfort to those who ask, according to the Scriptures.

The Lord will command His lovingkindness in the daytime; and His song will be with me in the night. (Psalm 42:8)

He will cover you with His pinions, and under His wings you may seek refuge; His faithfulness is a shield and bulwark. You will not be afraid of the terror by night, or of the arrow that flies by day. (Psalm 91:4–5)

If I say, "Surely the darkness will overwhelm me, and the light around me will be night," even the darkness is not dark to You, and the night is as bright as the day. Darkness and light are alike to You. (Psalm 139:11–12)

At night my soul longs for You, indeed, my spirit within me seeks You diligently. (Isaiah 26:9)

Arise, cry aloud in the night at the beginning of the night watches; pour out your heart like water before the presence of the Lord. (Lamentations 2:19)

In a like manner, faith is to the believer what the sniper-scope is to the soldier. Faith is the spiritual technology God gives to man. Faith gives believers the advantage "to see" in the dark. When you put on the goggles of faith, faith sends out the invisible, infrared rays of the substance of things hoped for. It goes out in front of you and reads present and future situations. When it comes back, the telescopic tube of the Holy Spirit converts it to the evidence of things not seen.

When my cancer caused all the physical weaknesses and painful adjustments, I had to learn how to use faith in order to see in the dark. I praise God that His presence always reassured me that He is just as much with me during "midnight situations" as He is with me during seasons of walking in the light.

FAITH WALK

The Bible is jammed full with accounts of people who learned to see in the dark through their faith goggles. In this midnight season, the Lord reminded me of Abraham's story in Genesis 12. God said to Abraham, "I want you to get out of your country; get out from among your kindred; get out of your father's house. I want you to go to a land that I will show you. And I will bless you, and I will bless those who bless you, and I will curse those who curse you, and I will make of you a great nation, and all of the nations of the earth shall be blessed through you." Hebrews 11:8–12 casts more light on Abraham's nightscope experience. "By faith, Abraham, when he was called, obeyed by going out to a place which he was to receive for an inheritance" (verse 8).

How was Abraham able to see in the dark? He heard God's command and he answered Him quickly. That blessed me. With all my heart I wanted to trust God every step of the way. As I staggered with a cane, as my voice quivered, as I had to be confined to a wheelchair, I still wanted to experience God in a fresh way. I didn't want to become bitter— I wanted to become better.

There are lessons that the Lord wants me to learn in this season, and I need His help to hold on—to see in the dark. He wants me to listen to Him and obey Him. He wants me to trust His heart even if I can't see His hand. His will was not that I be out of the dark but to trust Him for my midnight vision.

Going Deeper

1. Have you been feeling your way through life lately? In what ways do you feel like you're in the dark?

2. What steps of faith do you need to take even though you cannot see the next step?

3. What Scripture account has God used to remind you that He is with you in the dark?

The late Dr. Z. M. Bailey and
Mrs. Victoria Bailey-Curtis.

Pastor E.K. Bailey with his family-his wife,
Sheila, daughters Cokiesha and Shenikwa,
and son Emon.

Pastor E.K. Bailey with his late godfather,
the Reverend W.K. Jackson.

Pastor E.K. Bailey with his long-time
friend, the late Reverend E.V. Hill.

Pastor E.K Bailey with his mentors, Dr. C.A.W. Clark and Dr. Gardner Taylor.

Pastor E.K. Bailey with his dear friends Dr. A. L. Patterson, Dr. Henry Mitchell, and Dr. William Shaw.

Pastor Bailey with friend and
prayer partner Dr. Joel Gregory.

Pastor Bailey with his "son in the
ministry", Dr. Major Jemison.

The congregation of Concord Church voted unanimously
for Rev. Bryan Carter to succeed Dr. Bailey as pastor.

Pastor Bailey with long-time friend Rev. Jesse Jackson Jr.

Pastor Bailey and his wife Sheila with long-time friends, Hansel and Lillian Cunningham, and Martin Luther King III.

Pastor Bailey and Sheila with
friends Dr. Tony Evans and his wife, Lois.

Pastor Bailey and his wife Sheila, with the late
Dr. Stephen Olford and his wife Heather.

Dr. Bailey with his best friend of 35 plus years, Dr. M. V. Wade, at the "Celebrate the Recovery" service. Dr. Lloyd C. Blue is pictured in the background.

The men of Concord shaved their heads bald to show support for Pastor Bailey during his recovery.

The mask of assimilation placed on
Dr. Bailey before every procedure at M.D. Anderson.

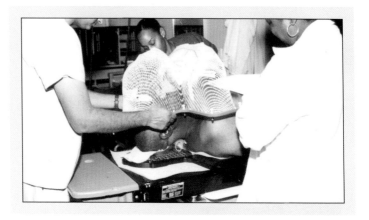

Dr. Bailey shown ringing
the bell celebrating the
last day of treatment with
family and friends.

Pray in the Spirit

on all occasions

with all kinds

of prayers and requests.

With this in mind,

be alert and always

keep on praying.

– *Ephesians 6:18* (NIV)

Chapter 8

GOD HEARS US WHEN WE CRY

Intimate Comfort from the Lord

*A*s the reality of the cancer settled in, so did the reality that I would never make it through this storm without God's presence. One of the joys of my life has been my devotional time and prayer time each day. I believe that a believer's life rises and falls around their devotional time with God. This illness was going to make that truth even more evident.

In fact, my cancer would require more faith, more obedience, and more time on my knees than ever before. This was sure to be an opportunity for God to do for me what Ryan's mother did for him (see "When the Storm Brews"): I needed God to stay with me as I weathered the winds and the waves of this tumultuous season.

❖ ❖ ❖

When the Storm Brews

One night while my young son, Ryan, was sleeping, a storm began brewing outside. After a loud clap of thunder, I heard Ryan wake up and run to find me. When I tucked him back into bed, he asked me to stay with him until he fell asleep. As I lay there with him, I realized Ryan hadn't asked me to make the storm go away, but to stay with him. How many times, I wondered, have I asked God to take away the storms of life, when instead, I needed to ask Him to stay with me and help me weather the storms more peacefully!

—AUTHOR UNKNOWN

This stormy season has shaped a different emphasis in my devotional life. I spend more time praising God for His character. The more I worship God for who He is, the less I think about my situation. I have developed a hunger for reading the Psalms. In the Psalms I find the greatest rest for my soul. As I nestle down in those pages, I become the deer that pants for the water brook in Psalm 42:1.

Throughout the day I will snack on Scriptures that comfort me and quiet my restless spirit. Before I know it, I find myself praying those Scriptures back to the Lord and enjoy the peace and freedom that comes from basking in His presence.

Here are a few passages that have become personal favorites. Read them and be reminded of God's majesty and might. Close your eyes and feast upon the promises that God has given us in His Word. Then look at seven more passages in "The Psalms on Trusting God's Goodness and Power." Next, build your own list of prayer verses. You are sure to find emotional healing, spiritual wholeness, security, and hope.

The earth is the Lord's, and all it contains, the world, and those who dwell in it; for He has founded it upon the seas and established it upon the rivers.

—PSALM 24:1

O Lord, our Lord, how majestic is Your name in all the earth.

—PSALM 8:1

I will give thanks to the Lord with all my heart; I will tell of all Your wonders. I will be glad and exult in You; I will sing praise to Your name, O Most High.

—PSALM 9:1–2

My soul finds rest in God alone; my salvation comes from him. He alone is my rock and my salvation; he is my fortress, I will never be shaken.

—PSALM 62:1–2 (NIV)

The Lord is my light and my salvation; whom shall I fear? The Lord is the defense of my life; whom shall I dread?

—PSALM 27:1–2

The more I read and meditate on the Scriptures, the more relief I experience. I may never know what it feels like to be pain free, but my focus is no longer on the pain. Peace has become my goal, and I find it by digesting the Word of God.

My heart leaps with admiration and gratitude when I consider God's love for me. The tension in my heart subsides when I focus less on my physical challenges. God has seemed very intentional about how He comforts me. He is showing Himself to be not only a Supreme God and the Lord of all but also my personal companion, my faithful friend, and my hiding place.

The Psalms on Trusting God's Goodness and Power

I love You, O Lord, my strength. The Lord is my rock and my fortress and my deliverer, my

God, my rock, in whom I take refuge; my shield and the horn of my salvation, my stronghold. I call upon the Lord, who is worthy to be praised. (18:1–3)

Do not hide your face from me, do not turn your servant away in anger; you have been my helper. Do not reject or forsake me, O God my Savior. . . . I am still confident in this: I will see the goodness of the LORD in the land of the living. Wait for the LORD; be strong and take heart and wait for the LORD. (27:9, 13–14 NIV)

Let integrity and uprightness preserve me, for I will wait for You. (25:21)

The Lord is my strength and my shield; my heart trusts in Him, and I am helped; therefore my heart exults, and with my song I shall thank Him. (28:7)

I waited patiently for the Lord; and He inclined to me and heard my cry. (40:1)

Great is the LORD and most worthy of praise. (48:1 NIV)

Serve the Lord with gladness; come before Him with joyful singing. Know that the Lord Himself is God. (100:2–3)

❖ ❖ ❖

BEING THANKFUL TO GOD

One day I recalled all the things that God had done for me over the years. My eyes filled up with tears as I jotted down some of the things that I am most grateful for. Cancer has a way of often blotting out all the blessings with which God fills our road of life. So I learned how to stop, pray, and reflect upon all that God gave me on the journey. I found sweet relief in writing prayers, prayer requests, and praise reports. In one journal entry I expressed my praise to and desire to focus on Him and His blessings:

> *Lord, there is much going on in my life right now. I don't know what to expect next, but I know that You are in the next moments of my day. It is so easy to concentrate on the things that may be in my days ahead. When I take my eyes off You, I feel burdened and frustrated. So, right now, I choose to concentrate on You. You have been too good to me to forget about the blessings with which You continue to shower me. I have preached for many years about Your power and Your healing touch. I know You can change my diagnosis if it is Your will.*

> *God, I desire that You will touch my body and make me whole again. I surrender to Your plan for my life. I know You are able to heal and restore me. Please come to me quickly. I know that I am in Your hands, but this experience is often frightening,*

Help me to count it all joy as I carry this pain. Thank You for showing me more about Yourself in my affliction. I want to concentrate more on You and less on my disease. Refresh me with Your Word, and comfort me with Your Spirit.

Thank You for hearing and answering my prayers. Lord, I submit my life to You.

Thank You, God, for being so good.

In another journal entry I listed the many blessings I had received:

Thank You for all of these wonderful blessings:

- *My salvation and eternal life through Your Son, Jesus*
- *Your unconditional love for me*
- *How You protect me from the snares of the enemy*
- *The fact that from this illness You will receive glory out of my life*
- *The Bible, a book that serves as my blueprint for daily living*
- *Your promise to be with me always*
- *The indwelling of the Holy Spirit*
- *My beautiful wife and caregiver, Sheila, who is an excellent home manager and a constant encourager.*

Sheila has been my most faithful friend and an incredible "copilot." She loves me lavishly and keeps me going with her smile, her touch, her service, and her push. Thank You for her sacrifices. I know that she gets tired, but she never makes me feel like I am a burden to her. Strengthen her, encourage her, and keep her grounded in You, Dear Father.

- *Allowing my daughter Cokiesha to use her writing gifts to be a blessing to me and this project. Her contagious laughter, love for God, and heart for people make my spirit so happy. Thank You for how You are growing her in faith. Her reliance on You blesses me.*

- *For my daughter Shenikwa. Watching her love for children makes me so happy. I am relieved that she didn't take my advice and become a lawyer. Teaching is clearly her passion. Her humor, fun-loving spirit, and serving hands keep my tank on full. I am so thankful for her commitment to serving our family.*

- *For my son, Emon, who is coming into his own. Thank You for how he is maturing. Thank You, God, for allowing him to carry on the Bailey name. I am so grateful for the son I prayed for. Thank You for how You are building his character as he watches how You protect and provide for his every need.*

- *Allowing me to be at M. D. Anderson. Only You could have worked this out. The excellent doctors and medical assistants provide me with outstanding care.*

- My preaching buddies around the country who are praying for me and encouraging their congregations to pray for me. Their outpouring of love continues to humble me.

- The two hundred charter members of Concord who trusted God's vision and started Concord with me over twenty years ago. I also remember Sister Blair, Brother Edmond, Brother and Sister Page, and all of the other saints who have joined the cloud of witnesses.

- The pastoral and administrative staff of Concord and the church leaders who continue to lead diligently despite my health challenges.

- The elders, staff, and members of Concord and the staff who love me and my family and pray for us regularly. They have made this journey joyful.

- For Brother Cunningham, Brother Spencer, Peach, Brenton, and all of the friends who are walking with me. Their care and concern continue to humble me. So do the caregivers, friends, and family who strengthen me with cards, letters, prayers, and the ministry of presence.

- The preaching partner that You have given me. Pastor Carter has made my load much lighter. His teachable spirit and compassionate way of serving has blessed me.

- Your promise in 1 Peter 5:10 that through suffering we are strengthened.

- *The fact that cancer can't destroy my hope in Jesus*
- *The birth of a passion to know You more intimately*

Just listing some of the things that I thank God for re-
leases an aroma that gives me an awareness of God's presence. The more I listed, the more God reminded me of
what He had already done in my life. I recalled what He
had done for His people hundreds of years ago. I re-
visited passages that recorded God's mighty acts throughout history. Psalm 90:1–2 took on a new meaning for me
as I read, "Lord, you have been our dwelling place in all
generations. Before the mountains were born or You gave
birth to the earth . . . from everlasting to everlasting, You
are God.

I knew the Lord already had established a perfect track
record. If He could deliver Daniel from the lions' den, then
surely He could hold me in His hands. Even if God decided not to spare my life, the Word of God gave me such
comfort that I could relax in Jesus' arms as He prepares
me for my new home in glory.

I desire that one day my name will be added to the "hall
of faith" with my foreparents who were able to endure
painful times for Christ's sake. May each of us experience
His peace in the midst of our storm. One song by Ray Boltz
and Lawrence Chewning, "The Anchor Holds," has been
an inspiration to me during this time as it reminds me that
God is our anchor.

I have journeyed through the long,
dark night out on the open sea

By faith alone, sight unknown;
Yet His eyes were watching me

And the anchor holds—
though the ship is battered

The anchor holds—
though the sails are torn

I have fallen on my knees
as I faced the raging seas

The anchor holds in spite of the storm

Going Deeper

1. In what way have you felt like "a battered ship"?

2. How has God's presence comforted you during this season?

3. Are you satisfied with the quantity and quality of time you spend in prayer and worship each day?

Although you or a loved one may be experiencing a painful season right now, you can still thank God for the things that fill your heart with gratitude and joy. Begin here:

Not to us, O Lord,

not to us,

but to Your name

give glory

because of Your lovingkindness,

because of Your truth.

—Psalm 115:1

Chapter 9

GOD'S SUPREMACY GIVES US PERSPECTIVE

Escaping the Trap of Self-Pity

As God was reminding me that He was with me, I picked up my journals again. It's been a lifelong habit to carry notepads with me. If I wasn't writing a sermon, I was recording my innermost thoughts. One day I was feeling pretty blue and couldn't stop the frustration from flooding my heart. I felt like the enemy was whispering in my ear things like, "Where is your God now, E.K.? Where was He when cancer crept into your body?"

Tears filled my eyes. As much as I love God, I wondered why this had happened to me and why God had pronounced such a judgment on my life.

It just so happened that when I was feeling this way, I found a yellow notepad journal that I had written nearly thirty years before. My heart landed on a page that included my testimony of being called to preach. Thinking back on those days, I remember it to be a season where I was in search of myself.

A REVEALING JOURNAL ENTRY

Although I have always been a man with passion, high energy, and an extrovert who lived to laugh and enjoyed discussing issues with people, I was very insecure. I was ordinary, but I desired to be extraordinary. Some of my friends were viewed as "the up-and-coming preachers of the next generation." They were so smart and did well in school. I had always hoped for a *C*. Some people graduated cum laude. Others, summa cum laude. I knew I would be graduating "Thank You, Lordy."

I wanted to be used by God. I wanted to make a difference. I wanted to prove the people wrong who thought I would fail. I wanted to be as good a preacher as my friends were. I wanted to be smarter. I wanted to make good of my father's name and legacy. I wanted to be a person whom God could trust. I wanted to be the best husband, the bravest and most compassionate father, and the most loyal friend. I wanted to be a great pastor and a prolific preacher.

Yes, and I admit it: I wanted the applause of people. I wanted recognition, and I wanted it often. All of those things were written in some implicit way throughout that journal.

The only theme that I could see flowing throughout that entire journal entry was, "I want, I need, I should, I will." I became embarrassed to see how much I thought about myself back then. Most of my requests centered on what I wanted. It seemed so strange that one moment I could feel confident, yet so insecure; humble, and yet arrogant; giving, yet selfish. Ambitious; yet so naive. I was inconsistent as could be.

But the notepad also reminded me of a special time that God had focused my thoughts on Him.

TIME TO REFOCUS ON GOD

Now so many years later, I needed Him to do it again. Cancer had consumed my thoughts with self-pity. God had put that remembrance in my hand to show me how self-centered my thinking was. I needed to refocus and to become God-centered again. In my heart of hearts, I sensed God saying, "It's not about you," but when those negative thoughts hopscotched all over my mind, I needed God to help me remember that He is sovereign and He can do whatever He wants. God was sending me a message.

He penetrated my thoughts with the profoundness of my struggle. I asked Him to forgive my doubts, and I thanked

Him for His great love for me. I praised Him that He thought enough of me to trust me with this pain. I asked Him to help me carry it humbly and graciously. Who am I to question God's ways? He is sovereign and can do *whatever* He wants, *whenever* He wants, and *however* He wants. He is God. What a remarkable wake-up call.

THE GOD WHO CHANGES HEARTS

Our loving God, who is full of grace, changed my heart years ago and was committed to changing me even now. The more I sat in God's presence, the easier it was to see how big He is and how small I am. I saw how valuable He is and how inadequate I am. I walked away from my quiet time with the Lord in tears because I had come to realize how wretched I was. How dare I think thoughts like, *How could I have cancer? I have too much work to do. People doing God's work don't get cancer!*

As I sat in our room at the Rotary House with a thermos of water and my Bible and journal in hand, I could feel God restructuring my character right there. He broke me in such a way that I saw my pain and suffering differently. Instead of wondering *Why me?* I began to think, *Why not me? I teach and preach the Word. Why would God not ask me to be an example? Why would He not ask me to carry pain in order to be perfected?* Throughout our treatment time in Houston, the Lord had been making me more sensitive to the needs of others and less concerned about myself.

I looked back at that old yellow notepad again. I saw a note that I had written some time ago as the Lord had spoken to me on this same issue. The note simply said, "E.K., find a cause that is bigger than you are. If you are your only cause, your cause is not big enough."

I remember the day He said that to me. In one of my weakest moments, God arrested me again with His love. When I was tempted to pity myself because I had cancer, God reminded me that this was not about me.

I was taking this illness personally. But as self-centered thoughts crept into my mind, God calmed me. My condition was not as bad as I thought; He allowed me to see patients who had worse side effects. He brought people to me who had lost loved ones and others who were sick, alone, and growing worse.

How could I be consumed with my cancer and my problems when there were other people around me who were worse and yet in better spirits? God asked me to remember His words on that day long ago: "E.K., find a bigger cause."

So I thanked Him for refocusing my thoughts on higher and bigger causes than myself. And I determined that the cancer would not accomplish five things, including destroying my faith. (See "Five Things Cancer Need Not Do.")

I had to tell myself over and over again: "It is not about me!" I repeated it until all the selfish thoughts brewing in my heart and mind dissipated.

Five Things Cancer Need Not Do

1. *Cancer need not destroy one's faith; neither should it keep you from dreaming, praying, worshiping, encouraging others, and having a plan of action that will impact the kingdom.*

2. *Cancer need not make you lose hope.*

3. *Cancer need not make you lose faith in God or cause you to question His love for you.*

4. *Cancer need not be given the energy that you could be using to help others who are worse off than you are.*

5. *Cancer need not become your disabler.*

—AUTHOR UNKNOWN

BACK TO THE CAUSE

Now that God had given me a rude awakening, it was time for me to get out of my emotional slump and get back to the greater cause.

Boy, was I happy to see how little I was and how big God was. Mrs. Charles Spurgeon once said, "Suffering is God's means of purifying us and bringing glory to Himself." What joy! God was purifying me! God was bringing glory to Himself! What a privilege!

Just like I was instructed to wear the "mask of assimilation" in order for the cancer cells to be zapped, God had to use His discipline and correction, guidance and love to zap some things in me that had given birth to sinful, selfish thoughts and ideas. With that in mind, God impressed upon my heart the need to share this cancer journey with others. He did not want me to throw in the towel because other people needed to see someone trusting God with complete control. People needed to see that God could make suffering and even death a sweet experience.

God said, "I allow this in your life so that you can bless someone else and so that I can change you." My attitude shifted from, "Why me?" to "Thank You for choosing me." God said, "I want other people to see in your example how I work mysteriously and powerfully. I want individuals and the body of Christ to deepen in their prayer life. I want more of you, E.K." Again, I thanked God for being a faithful Father.

I felt a renewed sense that the Bible was my blueprint for daily living with cancer. God's words cradled me like a baby in his mother's arms: "Call upon Me in [your] day of trouble; I shall rescue you, and you will honor Me"

(Psalm 50:15). It amazed me how God could give us a new disposition, a new way of thinking, and a new appreciation for Him.

When my throat was sore and raw from the radiation and I couldn't speak above a whisper, I said, "Lord, thanks that I am still alive, and I can still talk."

When I could no longer eat solid foods and they fed me through a tube, I said, "Lord, thank You that there is a way for me to get the nutrients I need."

When I wanted to go back to Dallas to get in my own bed, I stopped and thought, "You are providing for my daily needs. Thank You that Sheila and I are comfortable."

When I wanted to get back in Concord's pulpit, I had to say to myself, "I am so happy to be around other people who need to be encouraged. Lord, thank You for allowing me to learn the importance of preaching in my day-to-day activities. Thank You that we can live a sermon even when our lips can't preach one."

When Sheila and I became irritable, weary, and sick of being in the small suite, we prayed, "Lord, thank You that we have each other." And in this new season, Sheila continued to make lists of people that we could bless in some small way.

Isn't it just like God to intervene for us when we need Him to shift the gears to head in the direction that pleases Him?

TIME TO RING THE BELL

Time passed, and we got closer to our departure day from M. D. Anderson. I witnessed many patients participate in a bell-ringing ceremony. When a patient completed his or her last day of treatment, they were escorted to the gold bell fixed on the wall outside the radiation room. They were allowed to ring the bell so that people all over the hospital could hear the sound that represented life. To all of us, the bell-ringing day gave hope. I couldn't wait.

As my excitement grew, I was also very happy to hear about how Concord was doing back in Dallas. Every pastor wants his or her congregation to continue to grow. It made me happy to hear about the ministers who were preaching the Word and the people who were accepting Christ and joining the church. It confirmed what I always believed: The church belongs to God. The pastor is only an instrument. I could rest better, knowing that the church was in good hands because God has worked out the future, even if it did not include me. (Besides, it is not about me.)

The bell-ringing day was almost here; more about that in the next chapter. Even before our bell-ringing day, Sheila and I had become intentional about sending encouragement cards to other patients. And rooting for them on *their* bell-ringing days. We exchanged addresses so that we could keep in touch. Some of our new white friends had never before befriended African-Americans. Some of the patients we met had also met Christ. We spent quality time with people with whom we would have never met if our paths had not crossed at the hospital. We prayed for their healing. Many of them became our real-life heroes. We bonded with them, and they bonded with us. We thought less and less about our problems as we served others and sought causes that were bigger than us.

Clearly, it was not about us. It never had been. It's always and forever about Him!

Going Deeper

1. What part of your life did you feel like it was "all about you"? How has God shown you that it is all about Him?

2. In what ways have you developed a cause that is greater than you are?

3. Who needs your encouragement today?

The Lord

has done

great things

for us;

we are glad.

−*Psalm 126:3*

Chapter 10

GOD'S LOVE RESTORES OUR SOUL

Back to the Place of Promise

My bell-ringing day finally came! Our family, church members from Dallas, and friends from Houston greeted us in the hospital waiting room. Everyone smiled, whispered, and gave me "two thumbs-up." My heart was strengthened that so many people chose to be with us on the special day.

However, it was still a day that I had to receive treatment. Sheila and our children and the whole crew headed down to the room where they administered the radiation. The mood was bittersweet. I was happy that this would be the last time that I would have to wear that mask, lie on the table, and see the red lasers dashing across my upper body. But I was also saddened to say good-bye to some good people who had become my friends.

My mind went back to the first day when nervousness flooded my heart. I thought about the people who never got well, never finished their treatments, and never had an opportunity to ring the bell. My eyes filled up with tears. (I couldn't believe the crier I had become.) The fact that I was alive and strong enough to climb up on the cold table was a blessing in itself.

THE FINAL TREATMENT

As usual, they allowed me to play my favorite CDs throughout the treatment. I closed my eyes and worshiped God for the entire session. I talked to the Lord and told Him how much I appreciated Him being there with me and how grateful I was to be His son. I sang praises to His name. I promised Him that the days ahead would be filled with telling of His greatness. I vowed to spend the rest of my time on earth glorifying His name. My family watched as the session came to a close. They hugged one another, cheered for me, and thanked the staff.

When I got down from the table, they took the mask off for the final time. I stared in disbelief at how lifelike the image of my face was in the mask. Even now we have the mask on display in our home to remind us that God took a huge plastic mask, hundreds of red lasers, a cold table, and some chemotherapy in order to produce an image that He would be pleased with. As you endure illness or look out for someone who is sick, remember that through it all, God is shaping your circumstances and your character into a mold that looks like Him.

COME ON, RING THAT BELL!

Although I was as tired as usual after a treatment, my smile was hardly weary. I smiled like it was my birthday; I smiled brighter and wider as they rolled my wheelchair to the bell in the hallway. I reached toward the bell as cameras flashed and as people praised God right there in the hospital hallway.

I rang that bell like my life depended on it. Ring, ding! Ring, ding!

It was a beautiful sound in my ear—the sound of this season in my life coming to an end and of the glorious days ahead.

As we went down the hallway, we reached a big open area normally reserved for special programs. I couldn't believe it when I saw the faces of so many people from Dallas and Houston and hospital staff members holding up signs and banners that said, "We love you, Pastor!" "You did it!" "You're our hero!" "God is good!" and "We're proud of you!" They also displayed their love by wearing T-shirts that said, "E. K. Bailey Fan Club." I couldn't contain myself. The tears flowed again. They had planned a "Celebrate the Recovery" program and reception right there in the hospital. It was something I will never forget. Wow! What a day.

HOME AGAIN

We returned to Dallas to even more church members in our front yard welcoming us home. I had never been so happy to see our house, the home we moved into over twenty years ago. I saw our cat, our dogs, and our neighbors. It was good to be home.

We slowly got back into our routine. Sheila was great at administering the medicine, seeing after our family's needs, and tending to the people who called and came by to check on us. And I made myself at home again, set on recovery. As soon as I felt my strength returning, I began writing in my journal again:

> *Lord, it feels good to be back at home. Thank You!*

> *Thank You, Lord, that I can move around.*

> *Thank You for the fun we have as a family.*

> *Thank You for the many sons in the ministry who are committed to encouraging us. Thank You for Your faithfulness to me!*

At other times, my journal would look a little different:

I would give anything to preach again, Father.
Please allow me the strength to preach again. I still
don't feel strong enough. Please allow me to preach,
Jesus, even if I have to do it sitting in a chair.

Lord, I thought depression would subside once I
finished the chemo and radiation. Please help me
to crawl out of this pit. I feel like I'm in quicksand.
I don't know how to get out of the slump. Rejuvenate
my mind, please, dear Lord.

D IS FOR DEPRESSION

Although my battle with cancer had been fought, I still
faced periods of depression. According to one definition,
depression is "feelings of discouragement, hopelessness,
and a decline in energy, performance, and self-esteem."
Depression is caused by loss, stress, burnout, anger, and
abnormal body chemistry.

Of course, the most effective treatment for depression is
prayer. But don't neglect the physical either—try to get
consistent sleep, exercise, and vitamins. Be as mindful of
your own diet as you are of your ill loved one's. Indulge
in your favorite music and maybe even a massage now and
then too.

Please don't be ashamed or anxious about experiencing
these feelings and thus keep it to yourself; remember that

many of the great biblical leaders endured feelings of depression. (See "Who Experienced Depression?") Talk with someone who can help you deal with your problems with biblical principles, and, if needed, be open to medicine that can assist you. Write about them in your journal. In one entry I reminded myself and extolled God for His ability to change our moods: "God, thank You that You come to me when I need an awareness of Your presence. You are a mood changer and a mind regulator."

If you are caring for someone who is sick, you need to understand the stress you face when ministering to others. You are not superhuman, and it is okay to seek counsel from others and to read information so that you can learn how to cope with the intensity of your situation.

Who Experienced Depression?

- *Moses (Numbers 11:15)*
- *Jonah (4:3)*
- *Jeremiah (20:14–18)*
- *Job (23:8–10)*
- *David (Psalm 42)*
- *Habakkuk (1:2)*

WHAT'S NEXT?

What did God want me to do next? On my recovery bed, I wrote two books and journaled for possible additional books. My research assistant, Brenton Cross, was faithful as he helped me to get the books ready to be published. God even knows who to put in your life to help you accomplish His plans for you.

Next, God gave me the strength to preach again. Being back in the pulpit felt like being back home once more. In my first series, God led me to preach on marriage. What a mighty good time we had during those weeks. We truly heard from God, and the members really responded. Even single people said that they heard from the Lord on how to prepare for marriage and how to be a good steward of God's time.

It amazed me how He took my cracking voice and my deteriorating body and gave me the power to preach, teach, lecture, and share the gospel. That was the joy of my heart. Eventually, I felt weak again and could no longer preach. Then God took me from preaching with my lips to preaching with my life, and I was just as happy.

Through another preacher's sermon and through the ministry of the Holy Spirit in my study times, I learned three lessons from Psalm 126 that I believe will encourage anyone facing illness:

1. God will bring you back to the place of promise.

2. God will give you laughter and a song.

3. God gives us hope for a brighter future.

A SPRING SHOWER FOR MY SOUL

Then God brought me to Psalm 126, a great passage on restoration. Meditate on Psalm 126 for yourself:

> *When the Lord brought back the captive ones of Zion, we were like those who dream. Then our mouth was filled with laughter and our tongue with joyful shouting; then they said among the nations, "The Lord has done great things for them." The Lord has done great things for us; we are glad. . . . Those who sow in tears shall reap with joyful shouting. He who goes to and fro weeping, carrying his bag of seed, shall indeed come [home] with a shout of joy, bringing his sheaves with him.*

Those words were a spring shower to my soul. It continues to amaze me how God gives us the exact word to fit our predicament. We can be encouraged today that God promised to never leave us nor forsake us. He has given us a song. Even if you can't hold a tune in a bucket, God has placed a melody in your heart during this time.

As you walk this rocky road, God gives you hope for a brighter future. Maybe your future will be cancer and pain free. But even if it isn't, you still have a bright future. Don't dread tomorrow just because you're sick. Anticipate it, welcome it, and cherish it.

There will be a day when all who name the name of Jesus will enter into God's presence, and we will see Jesus face-to-face. We will take off this robe of mortality and put on immortality, and we will be changed, healed, and fully delivered (1 Corinthians 15:53). And our worship will have no end. We shall join with the cherubim and the seraphim as they shout, "Holy, Holy, Holy—Worthy! Worthy! Worthy!"

That is something that we can fix our hearts and minds on. That sounds like a bright future to me.

Going Deeper

1. What about your heavenly home makes you excited about entering eternal life?

2. What promises has God kept for you?

3. What about your future are you anticipating most?

Even though

I walk through

the valley of the

shadow of death,

I fear no evil,

for You are with me.

–Psalm 23:4

Chapter 11

THE LORD
IS OUR
SHEPHERD
Walking in the
Valley of the Shadow

O n schedule, Sheila and I went to the doctor's office for a checkup. I was happy to go back because I was ready to hear that my cancer was completely gone. After this visit, I would have to go only every three months for five years, and if no cancer reappeared, I would then be declared "cancer free."

When the doctor entered the room, however, I could tell that he did not have good news to share. The nasal passage and surrounding area was clear and the chemo and radiation eradicated all of the cancerous cells—that was good news. He then said, "But I am saddened to tell you that the cancer has spread to your lungs."

That's impossible, I thought. *How could this be? I am not a smoker. Maybe they made a mistake. Cancer doesn't even run in our family. I did everything that they asked me to. What went wrong? God, help me! Please, help me.*

I immediately asked what was the best treatment plan. Chemo again? Radiation? Surgery? Then in a serious, yet compassionate voice, the doctor said, "I'm sorry; we cannot cure this cancer. It will not respond to treatment."

I sat there stunned and bewildered. "No cure?" We then asked the dreaded question: "If there is no cure, then how long do I have to live?"

"You could have about six months to live," he answered. He said it in a calm and caring voice, but the words, "six months to live" couldn't possibly have been harder to hear.

MY RACING MIND

Six months. Six months? Six months! That's all that rang in my head at that moment. Then the reality. *I have so many things to do. I have so many people that I need to meet with. I have so much I need to tell my family. How do I break this news to my mother? How will my children react? God, what do I say to the church?* My feelings and my mind tried to outrace each other.

Sheila and I had learned so much about trusting God already in these last battles with cancer; I just couldn't give up on God even with this tragic news. I did have to ask God to quiet my restless spirit. There had to be a reason for this. But then I had to understand that God didn't have to tell me the reason. I said to myself and then to Sheila, "He is sovereign, and He can do whatever He wants, however He wants, when He wants."

After Sheila and I embraced and asked God to help us, we rode home teary-eyed, wondering what to do next. We decided that we would fight this pronouncement just as we fought the nasal cancer. If God's decision was to call me home, then we would accept His decision. On the other hand, if God chose to give me the strength to climb this Mount Everest, we would be faithful to Him on the journey.

I was surprised that Sheila and I felt stunned, but not faint. The last few months bonded us together in such a way that whatever came our way, we'd tackle it together. As much as I wanted to live, my desire was that my children's faith would be grounded and that they would not lose hope.

WE'VE GOT TO TALK

We called our children and family members, along with close friends over to the house. We sat in silence for a minute. Then, I mustered up the strength to say, "As you know, we met with the doctor today. The good news is that I don't have cancer in the nasal passage anymore, but the bad news is that the cancer has spread to my lungs." They sat quietly. When I tried to get the news out, I got choked up and began to cry.

One person asked, "Well, what do we need to do? What's the treatment for lung cancer?" I mark that moment as one of the most difficult in my life. Time stood still.

I wiped my face and cleared my throat and said, "They said I could have six months to live." They sat dumb-founded—astonished—by the doctor's report. They burst into tears and hugged one another. Obviously, shedding tears had become as familiar to us as breathing. But, we have found that in those tears God watered the dusty parts of our lives.

After we regrouped, I said to them, "We have always been a team, and we will continue to be one unified family. I know this is hard for us, but we must remember the God whom we serve. He is here with us and He will not leave us."

I couldn't believe the strength that God gave me to encourage them. Even in the midst of this new challenge, God was enabling me to be the leader, counselor, and pastor of my home. He wanted me to help them grow so that they would be prepared for the days ahead.

I wanted to live, but I resolved in my spirit that God could do to me whatever He wanted. I belonged to Him and I trusted Him.

MY JOURNAL

After we talked as a family, we called people with the news who would join us immediately in prayer. Then I grabbed my journal and wrote out everything that I was feeling. It felt good to release my emotions that were caged inside. The pen and the pad always helped me to unleash so many of my untamed thoughts. When I write them, I feel relief. I can look at the pad for days to come and be reminded of God's faithfulness. By writing I can be reminded of how far God has brought me. On those smooth, lined pieces of paper, I can prepare for the future . . . perhaps a future that I would not be part of.

As I look back, this particular journal entry stuck out:

Things to Do:

- *Talk to Cokiesha, Shenikwa, and Emon. Tell them that if this cancer is what takes my life, do not think for one second that this means that their lives are over.*

- *Ask the girls not to rush into getting married just because I am sick. God will be their covering.*

- *Talk to the family about the importance of taking care of their bodies by eating right and exercising.*

- *Spend more time writing books.*

- *Read more on lung cancer and alternative medicine.*

- *Talk to the staff about my new diagnosis.*

- *Talk to the congregation about the new diagnosis and preparing to receive a new leader if God should take me home.*

- *Teach more on how cancer affects the church community.*

- *Tell family not to keep bad news from me just because I am sick . . . God will help me deal with bad news.*

- *Make sure the insurance policy and will are in order so the family won't have that kind of strain.*

Family Losses

Sometimes our losses seem too frequent and too heavy. After the doctor declared that cancer had entered my lungs, I realized my heavy heart had endured many losses in the past two years.

My wife lost her mother, Mrs. Lucy Smith. I lost three of my close friends. Then the biggest blow: I lost my mother, Mrs. Victoria Curtis, and my godfather, Dr. W. K. Jackson.

During that time, there is sorrow but there is also solace. God has promised that He "is faithful, [and He] will not allow you to be tempted beyond what you are able . . . to endure" (1 Corinthians 10:13). He helps us to endure.

Remembering that this cancer was not about me, I kept looking for ways to help other people as I battled this deadly disease. Sure, the pain seemed unbearable at times. My skin became ultrasensitive, so it hurt when people wanted to give me a handshake or a hug. My skin also couldn't tolerate drafts, so we had to keep the house very warm. My heart was heavy at times when I thought about the emotional burdens of the last two years.

It seemed like our family was walking through the valley of the shadow of death.

Going Deeper

1. If you could see your future, how would you and your family handle your last days on earth?

2. As you have been dealing with your illness, what blows have you experienced that made your road harder to travel?

3. If you had to make a "Things to Do" list during your last days, what would be on it?

Those who go down

to the sea in ships,

who do business

on great waters;

they have seen

the works of the Lord,

and His wonders in the deep.

—Psalm 107:23-24

Chapter 12

GOD HOLDS US UP
Developing Deep-Water Faith

I have spent all of my adult life teaching and preaching the power of God. I've exhausted myself encouraging people to get out of the comfortable boat and to step out into the water of impossibility. Now God had charged me with the same task of getting out of the shallow water of life. God wanted me to develop a deep-water faith.

Shallow water is when everything is fine and we're feeling our best. It's easy to trust God in the shallow water. However, God wants to know if we will trust Him when the winds blow and the seas churn. I empathized with the disciples' fear that night on the boat when Jesus was sleeping (Mark 4:37). Huge waves beat against the boat. The lightning cracked and flashed bright and never came to an end. The boat rocked with the wind to such an extreme that it might capsize with the next wave.

DEEP AND BEAUTIFUL

In the days after the doctor's prognosis, I felt the waves beating so hard against my boat that I didn't think I could withstand it. I was in deep water.

As frightening as it was, I thought about the striking difference between deep and shallow water. I thought about the potential danger of diving into the shallow water and how limited people are who never learn how to swim in the deeper water. And though we can see the pretty and colorful fish that swim in shallow water, the great fish make the deep water their home. Then I thought about what takes place in the shallow parts of the ocean and in the deep parts of the sea.

It hit me. As in life, there is no challenge in shallow water. At fifty-eight years old, I recognized that a life without challenge is a life without substance—without strength—without growth. As we who have been appointed to bear an illness in our bodies, God wants us to stop being afraid of life's deep water. He dwells in those waters too. It's there in those waters that He challenges our faith and causes us to grow. It's there that He will hold us up.

I've felt like that on my journey before. As a young pastor I felt God leading me to organize the Concord Church. I wanted to heed the call, but where would we get the money? Who would follow me? Would they trust someone half their age to lead them? God nudged me and whispered, "Get out of the boat." On another occasion I sensed God calling me to deep water when I decided to pursue a doctorate degree. How could I pastor the church in Dallas, spend time with my family, and earn a doctorate degree at the same time? God whispered, "Deep water."

Other times, I remember being afraid as I watched my children suffer. Cokiesha experienced a bad burn on her head before she was two years old. Doctors had to remove all of her hair. They simply said to us, "Buy her a bonnet. She probably will not grow hair again." Then, my son, Emon, accidentally cut himself on the face. Trying to be like Daddy, he grabbed a razor in the bathroom and mimicked me shaving and cut himself near his eye.

We didn't know what would become of either situation, but as we trusted God with our children, He whispered, "I am in control." Even when I heard the terrible news of cancer for the first and second and third time, God impressed upon me His desire for me to trust Him no matter how desperate the situation appeared to be.

DEEP WATER AND MATURING

As patients and caregivers, we hear God whisper to us, "For what I have called you to do, you must get out of your comfort zone." He wants to mature us. At times, He maximizes our growth by getting us out into the deep water. A poet, Robert Browning Hamilton, said it better:

> *I walked a mile with Pleasure,*
> *She chatted all the way;*
> *But left me none the wiser*
> *For all she had to say.*
>
> *I walked a mile with Sorrow*
> *And ne'er a word said she;*
> *But, oh, the things I learned from her*
> *When Sorrow walked with me!*[1]

God wants us in deep water to challenge our faith.

DEEP WATER AND COMMITMENT

We don't really think about that when people are forcing us to take medicine all day long. That never crosses our mind when we are encouraged to change our diets. We never consider what we can learn during the times in life when things are unpleasant and uncomfortable. In shallow water, you can do a lot of things that you cannot do in deep water. In shallow water, you can jump in and do your thing. But in deep water, you can't fool around with your feelings.

You have to have a commitment to make it in deep water. He wants you in deep water so that He can increase your commitment.

❖ ❖ ❖

Thanking God
During the Deep Waters

When we realize the deep-water experiences can increase our commitment, encourage change, and bring God's biggest blessings, we can thank Him during those deep, trying waters. Here's part of a thanksgiving prayer I gave the Lord one day:

Thank You for being my Rock, my Sustainer, my Deliverer. I worship You because of who You are. Thank You for Your great and unconditional love. Thank You for Your promise to never leave me nor forsake me. I confess to You that I find myself looking away from You from the shallows and fixing my eyes on things that I cannot control. Please help me to surrender to Your plan for my life. Thank You for hearing my prayer. Thank You for the gift of Your presence in the deep water. I promise to trust You more, even when I am afraid. Where there is doubt and fear in my life, O God, please give me faith and confidence in You. I know that You will be a lamp that guides my feet in this dark and benighted world. In Jesus' name, amen.

DEEP WATER AND CHANGE

Shallow water doesn't require much change. In fact, the most radical thing you can do in shallow water is put on a bathing suit. But you will need more than a bathing suit when you get in deep water. Down in deep water, the pressure gets heavy.

There are two kinds of people in the world—those whose lives are controlled by pressure from without and those whose lives are controlled by power from within. You are going to get the pressure. God wants you in deep water so that He can teach you how to dress for receiving the power to change—a spiritual power that comes from within.

We protect ourselves in deep water with the armor of God (Ephesians 6:10–18). I know, armor should drag you down in water. But this spiritual armor floats! It lifts our spirits and protects against the waves.

Can you imagine tackling cancer without being "dressed" appropriately? I would have looked ridiculous getting on the medical table at M. D. Anderson without the mask of assimilation. The doctors told me that it protected me.

Without it, I would have been injured, and the cells may not have been attacked properly.

The same is true in life. You and I have to be appropriately adorned for the task that God has given us. Indeed, God is at His best in deep water. Psalm 107:23–24 says, "Those who go down to the sea in ships, who do business on great waters; they have seen the works of the Lord, and His wonders in the deep."

Amazing Truths

From the Beatitudes to the humiliation of the cross, Jesus teaches us that the kingdom of God is often different than we might think with our finite and carnal minds. Here are some amazing truths about the deep:

- *If you want to see the works of God, you have to get out of shallow water.*

- *Put on the armor of God, and you will float on the water.*

- *God wants us to stop fearing life's deep waters—He dwells there.*

- *You never find any of God's big blessings in shallow water.*

- *In the deep, you must be willing to trust God.*

God chooses not to do much in shallow water; we have too many props around us, and God knows our nature. We would give the credit to the prop that held us up. If we had it our way, we would tell people, "Yes, I did this and this and that, and that's how I dealt with my cancer." Or we would impress others by saying, "I was diagnosed, but after seeking treatment at this place and with this doctor, I was cured." But, sometimes, God allows us to experience deep water with our health so that no would can get any credit but Him.

GOD'S BIG BLESSINGS

I am not a fisherman, but I have heard what people catch in shallow water—minnows, trash, and tennis shoes. You never find any of God's big blessings in shallow water. They won't fit in shallow water.

Can you imagine us being in heaven and God showing us a gift that He wants to give us? Can you see us saying, "That is exactly what I wanted. Why didn't I ever get it in life?"

Then God says, "Do you see the size of that blessing?"

"Yes, God."

"That blessing wouldn't fit in the shallow water you stayed in. You never got out far enough in order for Me to send that blessing to you. You stayed in shallow water."

Our challenge is to not allow cancer or any illness to force us to stay in shallow water. We must be willing to trust God in the deep.

Our character will develop in deep water.

Our patience will develop in deep water.

Our attitudes will be reconstructed in deep water.

Our appreciation for the people in our lives will be developed in deep water.

And, yes, our blessings will surface as we trust God in the deep water.

Ignoring the requests of your doctor is for shallow-water Christians. Being hard to get along with as your caregiver tries to make you comfortable is for shallow-water Christians. But trusting God in the deep water, the area where we are most uncomfortable, is where we will learn how to trust God. He won't abandon us in the deep water, but He also can't teach us to swim if we never get out of the boat.

He wants to take people like you and me out of the shallow water and into the deep. He did it for Abraham; he was a deep-water man. Hannah was a deep-water woman. Paul was a deep-water man, but most of all, Jesus was a deep-water Man. One Friday, with a cross on His shoulder, He walked out in deep water. He hung on that cross, died, went in the grave, but early Sunday morning, He got up with all power.

If you go in the deep, He won't leave you there. He'll show up, and when He shows up, He'll show out.

Going Deeper

1. Do you enjoy swimming, scuba diving, snorkeling, or jet skiing? Have you always been water friendly?

2. What about that sport (or sports) causes you to see how God keeps us afloat in life?

3. What amazes you the most about the water? Journal about how God has held you up in the ocean of life.

NOTE

1. Robert Browning Hamilton, "Along the Road," http://www.worldofquotes. com/author/Robert-Browning-Hamilton/ 1/index.html

There was

given me a

thorn in the flesh,

a messenger of Satan

to torment me—

to keep me

from exalting myself!

–2 Corinthians 12:7

Chapter 13

GOD'S GRACE MEETS US IN OUR PAIN
The Ministry of the Thorn

*W*hen the emotional pain and mental anguish seem unbearable, I cry out to the Lord. He always comforts me with a Scripture, a song, a card, a friendly visitor, or a story.

One day a young man, Ron, was swimming at the beach, and his friend watched him from the shore. Somehow Ron couldn't swim back, and he began to drown. He went up and he went down; up and then down. As Ron bobbed in the waves, he saw his friend at the edge of the water. He wondered why his friend would not jump in and save him. Little did Ron know that his friend was aware that if he had attempted a rescue now, they both would have died because the swimmer was fighting the water.

Frantic and without pausing, Ron thrashed the water. Soon the swimmer ran out of energy, and he did the "dead man's float." Then, fast and furiously, the friend jumped in and saved him.

Sometimes God waits for us to exhaust ourselves before He jumps in. It's only when we do the "dead man's float" that many of us will allow God to save us. I had reached a point in my life where I was facedown in the water. No medicine or cure could rescue me. Told that I had only six months to live, all I could do was wait to see how God was going to save me.

God rescues some of us by healing us. He rescues others with medication or surgery. Often, however, God chooses death to rescue us from pain and suffering. No matter what He chooses, He receives the glory.

A BADGE OF IDENTITY

The Lord allowed me to understand that sometimes our affliction is our badge of identification with Jesus. God allows the "ministry of the thorn" to authenticate our witness for Him. It doesn't matter if our affliction is our health, our finances, our relationships, or some personal circumstance; we all have a thorn. How are you handling your thorny situation?

The apostle Paul explained his thorny situation: "There was given me a thorn in the flesh, a messenger of Satan, to torment me—to keep me from exalting myself" (2 Corinthians 12:7). Paul used his physical realities to indicate a spiritual work.

Paul wrote candidly about the thorn. He explained how uncomfortable it was, but he also told of the benefits of the thorn. It is important that you and I remember the benefits of physical ailments—even cancer—when we feel the thorn digging in.

In the midst of discomfort, we still have a responsibility. We have to understand that afflictions do not prevent effectiveness. A lot of people think that because they are having afflictions or trouble in the home and all kinds of problems that they can't serve the Lord. But trouble at its worst is still just trouble. It does not make you ineffective, because your effectiveness is not based on your ability. Your effectiveness and mine are based on God's ability.

Moses almost missed the trip down to Egypt, saying, "I can't talk right . . . I stutter." I imagine the Lord said, "I know your weaknesses. I made you. I made your mouth. I made all of you. I know that you have a speech impediment, but, Moses, your problem is that you don't understand that I don't need your ability. What I need is your availability. I can put My ability into your availability."

We also need to understand that afflictions serve us in a positive way. Afflictions lift us to a new dimension of living that we would never reach if it were not for the afflictions.

BOUNTIFUL GRACE

Just as important, our afflictions drive us to God, and He meets us with His grace.

You may not feel like you have everything that you need right now, but guess what you do have enough of? God's grace. His grace is sufficient for you. He speaks to you in your affliction, and He has promised to be strong when you are weak (2 Corinthians 12:9).

Our willingness to bear afflictions shows our love for God. Isn't God worth the pain?

God isn't asking us to do something new. His Son, Jesus, had to endure the ministry of the thorn. Friday night looked like a lost cause, but Friday's darkness turned into sunshine on Sunday morning. The confusion on Friday was turned into understanding on Sunday. The despair of Friday was turned into hope one Sunday morning. The same grace that saved you will walk with you. He'll talk with you. He'll tell you that He is your very own.

Going Deeper

1. Have you ever poked yourself on the thorn of a rose? Did that turn you away from enjoying the beauty and touch of roses?

2. How has the ministry of the thorn affected the way that you view God, our Life Gardener?

My grace
is sufficient.

–2 Corinthians 12:9

Chapter 14

OUR GOD
IS FOREVER
THE SAME

Trusting Every Moment to Him

*I*n the introduction I noted that the title of this book came from a sermon preached by Dr. Robert Smith a few summers ago. "Farther In and Deeper Down" turned flips in my spirit, for as I sat there listening, God flashed images across my mind—images of my past, images of my present, and images of my future.

I looked up and told the Lord, "Thank You." I had to tell Him how much I appreciated His transforming power in my life.

I sensed the Lord tell me more work had to be done and that He wanted me to be in it for the long haul. Even with cancer, God expected me to give Him my best. He wanted the best of my worship, the best of my talents, the best of my time, and the best of my choices. He wanted the best that I could offer Him. Besides, He deserved my best.

He promised that as I gave Him my best, He'd give me His best. As I stood up for Him, He'd stand up for me. He wanted to make me just like His Son, Jesus.

"AM I THERE YET?"

Throughout my life I never knew how far God wanted me to go, but every time I had sacrificed or endured pain for Christ's sake, I would look at Him and say, "Am I there yet?" God would look back at me and say, "Go farther." I kept digging and digging until I thought I had reached the place where God desired for me to be. God said again, "Go farther." Sometimes I would think to myself, *Lord, I can't go any farther.* He would lovingly and directly reply, "Go deeper."

I would work and look back at Him for a sign of approval, but He'd say, "Go farther in and deeper down, My child." I'd work harder and sweat more profusely. Still He would say, "Not yet. Dig deeper."

Then, one day I understood where this was going. I would be digging deeper and going farther until the day that I finished my work here on earth.

Jessica McClure was almost two years old when she went farther in and deeper down. She sat in her aunt's backyard in Midland, Texas, dangling her feet over what seemed to have been a harmless ground depression. Her aunt left her only for a few moments, but that's all it took. Jessica attempted to stand up and suddenly fell twenty-two feet into an abandoned water-well shaft.

A rescue team was dispatched with heavy equipment, and for the next fifty-eight hours, they worked feverishly to dislodge Jessica from the abandoned shaft.

Robert O'Donnell was assigned as the primary rescuer. After drilling a parallel shaft thirty feet down and then digging five feet across through sheer rock, they lowered O'Donnell. When O'Donnell had descended and maneuvered his way across the five-foot tunnel, he was able to touch Jessica's body. He was able to even get her vital signs.

However, just as everything appeared to be going so well, disaster struck. As Mr. O'Donnell reached for Jessica, she slipped farther down the shaft. They pulled O'Donnell out of the shaft to recast their strategy. The pediatricians told them, "Whatever you're going to do, do quickly, for she can't last much longer."

In a very short time, they put O'Donnell back down into the shaft. This time, when he reached little Jessica, he heard a voice from the top that cried out, "O'Donnell, pull hard. You may have to break her in order to save her." O'Donnell was afraid because he knew how fragile the two-year-old girl was. But complying with the direction from above, he pulled hard.

As he pulled, little Jessica began to cry. Can you imagine how his heart broke? He pulled hard, so hard it messed up one of her toes, but he kept on pulling. He pulled hard until it scratched up her face, but he kept pulling. He made one last tug, and her body was dislodged from the shaft. He put her in the rescue apparatus, and the rescue team pulled her up to safety.

THE SCAR THAT SAVES

They had to amputate one toe, but nobody said O'Donnell was too tough. She had to have oxygen, and today she has a scar on her forehead, but nobody said he was too harsh. Everybody knew that if he did not scar her, he would not save her.

God showed me how we are not much different from beautiful baby Jessica. Every now and then, God has to pull hard. He may cause us to amputate some things. He may even scar us up a little bit, but God knows if He doesn't pull hard, if He doesn't scar us, He may not save us. We may have to endure the side effects of chemotherapy and the hair loss involved with radiation, but that is His way of saving us. We may even have to accept that death is closer than we'd like for it to be, but that could be God's way of healing us.

THE MYSTERY OF SUFFERING

Second Corinthians reminds us of the importance of going farther in and deeper down. In chapter 12:1–10, God shows us how we can go farther in and deeper down with Him. As we sweat and work diligently, God calls us into the mystery of suffering. God uses suffering to take us farther in and deeper down.

As we look out across the landscape of our human existence, we see suffering everywhere—in our homes, in the faces of ailing loved ones, on the news, and in our hospitals. We even see it in ourselves, as our bodies break down under the weight of time.

We ask the question, "Why—why me?"

What we discover is that suffering is shrouded in the veil of mystery.

Suffering disciplines our moral choices. Before God created the world, He created angels; later God created earth and man and woman. He gave them something that He didn't give to angels. He made us free moral agents. We are free to enthrone God or dethrone God.

Satan acted to dethrone God. Adam decided to follow Satan's pattern. Our ancestors who were preachers used to say,

When man sinned, he fell from essence to existence.

When man sinned, the lion jumped on the lamb.

When man sinned, the dog barked at the cat.

When man sinned, the grass turned brown.

When man sinned, the leaves turned brown and fell from the trees.

When man sinned, the oceans started throwing hurricanes at the land.

Sin affected all of nature.

Sin affected all of our relationships. When man sinned, it opened the door to suicide, homicide, and fratricide. When man sinned, it disturbed the relationships of everything in this world.

Therefore, God, in His infinite wisdom, uses suffering to discipline our morality. As I have said to my congregation frequently, God uses the spade of sorrow to dig the well of joy. Oswald Chambers says, "You can't drink grapes; they must be crushed."

❖ ❖ ❖

Why Do We Suffer?

Why we suffer a particular hardship remains a mystery. Yet the Bible makes clear people suffer on earth for several reasons, any one or more of which may apply in our present situation.

We suffer:

1. *to go farther in and deeper down with God. He can draw us closer to Him during our pain.*

2. *to discipline our morality. Suffering is a key outcome of sin.*

3. *to disciple our mortality. We are frail and have limits, and suffering reminds us we have nothing that lasts except Him.*

4. *to put our hope in Jesus, not in doctors, treatments, or even our pastors.*

But not only does God use suffering to discipline our morality; God uses suffering to define our mortality. Sometimes we get so comfortable in our nice homes, good jobs, fine cars, and influential circles that God allows suffering to remind us that we're nothing without Him.

Sometimes we can get in the position of surpassing greatness. We get a false impression of who we really are. God sometimes allows cancer to remind us that we need Him. Sometimes God allows us to go farther in and deeper down so that we may spend more time with Him. As Christians, it is so easy to let the pastor do everything. We let the pastor do our praying for us. We let the pastor do our Bible study for us. We let the pastor do our worship for us. At times, God says "I'm going to allow pain to enter into your body so that you will spend quality time with Me." Sometimes God allows pain just to remind us that we won't be here forever.

People come and people go, but the Bible says "Jesus is the same yesterday and today and forever" (Hebrews 13:8). As we suffer, we will be challenged to not put our hope mainly in our doctors, our treatments, our caregivers, our spouses, or even our pastors or other spiritual leaders. God asks us to put our hope in Jesus.

HIS SUFFICIENT GRACE

The effects of our suffering all depend on how much we crawl up in the Master's lap and allow Him to minister to us. God says to you and me what He said to Paul, "My grace is sufficient" (2 Corinthians 12:9). Sometimes we think that just because we ask God to heal us that He will take the disease away. He has the power to do that, and sometimes He does, but He can also choose to say, "No, My grace is sufficient."

How do we deal with that? We are to receive His grace. Grace means getting what you need when you don't deserve it. Grace means overshadowing mercy. Grace means getting God's extraordinary goodness. "I'm gong to give you My grace, and My grace is sufficient." Sufficient means "aplenty." Sufficient means enough, more than you can use, continually available to you.

God did not give Paul what he asked for, but He gave him something better. Paul asked for relief, but God gave him grace. Have you been focusing so much on your physical relief that you have forgotten to ask God for His grace?

DYING GRACE

I know, it's easy to forget to ask for grace when we so desperately want relief, but God's Word encourages us to receive God's unlimited grace. When I was at my first pastorate, I remember so vividly going over to an elderly member's house. When I got there, she was sitting up smiling. The family had told me that she was near death, so I went in expecting her to be moaning and groaning. When I got there, she said, "Hi, Pastor. How're you doing?"

"I'm fine. How are you?"

"It's so good to see you. You know, I've been on this road a long time, but it won't be long before I see Jesus!"

That's what she told me. "I can't wait to see my Master's face!" I went to encourage her, but she ended up encouraging me.

God had given her something that He hadn't given me. God gave her dying grace. She had grace to do what I didn't have grace to do because it wasn't my time. A lot of the members of the church have said to me, "Pastor, thank you for being so strong." It is not because I am so strong; it is because God has given me His grace.

The apostle Paul, who suffered plenty, said, "Therefore I am well content with weaknesses, with insults, with distresses, with persecutions, with difficulties, for Christ's sake" (2 Corinthians 12:10). Like He did with Paul, God wants to take us farther in and deeper down into the victory of suffering. We normally don't look at suffering as being something that gives us victory, do we?

FIRST A TEST, THEN THE TESTIMONY

None of us can receive victory without suffering. The catchy cliché "You can't have a testimony without a test" is so true. We can never appreciate our health unless we know what it feels like to be sick. We could never appreciate the ability to walk or talk or drive or stand if we never had to depend on water thermoses to keep our mouths moist, or a cane or wheelchair to support us. But God encourages us to adopt Paul's attitude when he said, "I'm well content in my weakness. I can handle insults, distresses, persecutions, difficulties, pain, and even death because I know it's all about God and not about me."

I am not suggesting that we pretend that we like the pain or that we have to pretend that we are not ill. I am simply suggesting that we acknowledge our pain to the Lord and still say, "When I am weak, He is strong."

A Deep Well

Cancer patients, we need a deep well to handle our dry seasons. If we stay on the surface, we'll be shallow in our lives. If we stay on the surface, we'll wither in the dry wind, but if we keep on digging—digging into the Word of God, digging into our prayer lives, digging into blessing other people—when the dry season comes, we'll be deep enough to have cool water coming out from a ready well.

It would be so easy to close this book by telling you to take my word for it, but my word isn't good enough. I encourage you to look at how Jesus kept digging as He headed toward Calvary. He knew that no other mountain to carry the sinner would be deep enough, and He kept on digging. He dug till He hit redemption. He dug till He hit salvation. He dug till He hit justification.

He kept on digging. He dug till He hit a second chance. He dug till He hit mercy. He dug till He hit grace. He dug until He closed His eyes and bowed His head and died for you and me.

Then, God said, "That's deep enough!"

Epilogue

RIDING
THROUGH
THE STORM

By Sheila M. Bailey

The day began as any other day in the hospital—doctors and medical staff making their routine calls, including examining my husband of thirty-four years. When I accompanied the oncologist to the hall, he invited me into the consultation room. I had been to that room before, having cookies and punch during gatherings for families of patients, but I had never been invited there by E.K.'s oncologist before.

My heart beat faster. Perhaps there had been a turn of events, or perhaps there was a new drug that would improve his condition. The expression on his face was that of compassion, but it didn't indicate that he was the bearer of such good news.

How often had my husband said in sermons, "You need an inner brace for outer circumstances." Quickly and quietly I prayed, "Lord, give me a calm, quiet spirit so I won't panic. Prepare me for what has been prepared for me."

The doctor softly but authoritatively said, "He could have less than two weeks."

I felt as though I had been suddenly anesthetized, emotionally numbed. While tears were streaming down my cheeks, the nurse rushed in to tell me to hurry to his room. Immediately I joined my daughters, son, and the male caregiver. My husband was unresponsive. The nurse instructed us to talk to him because the last sense to leave as one is dying is their hearing. With a sense of urgency, we all started saying how much we loved him and what he meant to us.

Instantaneously, he opened his eyes, startled by all of us. Later I learned through the palliative care guide that when a patient is in the final stages, it may not appear that he is dying.

A few weeks later, October 22, 2003, E. K. Bailey took his last breath and died in the Charlton Methodist Hospital, Dallas, Texas.

Many people have asked me to describe what it was like to accompany my husband on this pilgrimage. Maybe glimpses into our lives will prepare you for whatever storms come into your life. E.K. would say, "You are either leaving a storm, in a storm, or headed toward a storm." Whatever the storm you may experience, Jesus is the only One who says, "Peace; be still!"

Remember the basics. God loves you with a passion. You have His presence, promises, and provisions. God will do a new thing with you.

How often after hearing my husband preach one of his signature sermons had I meditated on Philippians 3:10 and said, "I want to know You in the power of Your resurrection and the fellowship of sharing in Your sufferings, becoming like You in Your death."

When I reflected upon my life, it became apparent that I wanted the power of the Resurrection while wanting to negotiate a degree of suffering. I was quick to verbalize, "Take this cup from me." Then cautiously I added, " . . . not my will, but Yours be done." With each cancer, the tears flowed more when I said, "Not my will, but Yours be done." The doctor told us the first time it was renal cell carcinoma. Four years later we were told it was nasopharyngeal carcinoma, and in six months we were told it had metastasized to the lungs. At that point I was tempted to say, "Enough of the suffering! I need some Resurrection power." I felt as if the bottom had fallen out from underneath me, and I wasn't on a ride at the amusement park. It was *real*!

DRAW FROM THE WELL

The validity of E.K.'s often spoken words gripped me: "The time of examination is not the time for preparation! Testing time is not prepping time!" It wasn't time for enrolling in Bible study. It was time to call on the name of the Lord and draw from the well of experiencing God. It was time to bring my behavior in line with my beliefs. It was time for the Scriptures, the legacy of prayer, faith, courage, and discipline that were extended to me from my deceased parents and spiritual mentors to come forth in me. Immediately, I recalled that faith and fear could not occupy the same space, so I chose faith.

I reflected on people in the Bible who trusted in God. I then began to personalize the life of Hannah, who had sorrows (although different from mine). She offered supplications to God, waited for God to answer her prayer, and made sacrifices by keeping her vow to the Lord. God transformed a sorrowful woman into a singing woman in the very next chapter. Psalm 31 is interwoven with the psalmist's praise, plight, petitions, provisions, and promises to persevere. Lord, I want to be like the psalmist.

Jesus, the Great Physician, was the only One who could handle my husband's negative report. So our pilgrimage was punctuated with prayer, physicians, and every provision imaginable.

After the first diagnosis, we told our family and asked some of the church leaders to come to the house to pray with us. After the second diagnosis, we had our family and leaders come to pray. After the third diagnosis, family and leaders came to pray again. This was only the beginning of an intense prayer effort coordinated by our prayer coordinators, Rev. Rick Jordan (our brother-in-law) and Cedric Jordan. The church had prayer meetings at 6 a.m., noon, and 7 p.m. People were encouraged to pray all during the day for healing of their senior pastor and others who needed healing. Prayer needs were on our Web site. People throughout the country and even in other countries were praying, "Lord, do it for us."

The kidney cancer was the first, corrected by surgery; he healed and continued preaching and pastoring. Our church, Concord Baptist, moved into a new worship facility two months after his surgery. What a blessing!—a new beginning for the preacher/pastor and a new beginning for the congregation. Four years later he started having ear problems; we received the report that he had cancer in the nasal passage on our son's birthday. It was a challenge to celebrate our son's birthday when my husband's life was being threatened with a terminal illness.

FIND ANSWERS TO YOUR QUESTIONS: RESEARCH

Questions raced through our minds: Nasopharyngeal carcinoma—What is it? When we heard that it was prevalent among Asians and smokers, it baffled us! He is neither one. How do you pronounce it? How do you spell it? How is it treated? What are the best resource centers? What is the survival rate? What stage is he in? Where do we begin? Who will be the doctors?

Research is important in understanding and accepting a terminal illness. Our research began with my family sitting around my sister's computer as she and her husband surfed the Internet. Others joined us in acquiring a wealth of information.

A month before the diagnosis, I was invited to speak at a women's conference. I heard Mona Tuma tell of her multiple experiences with cancer. I had no idea that God would connect us again in a very remarkable way. The Lord brought her back to my remembrance. We met again, and she was a gold mine of inspiration and information. Her book, *Bouncing Back Again . . . and Again . . . and Again,* continued to take us farther in and deeper down as it led us through Bible study on choosing to face life anyway, daring to trust again, and learning to laugh again and live. There were self-study exercises, discussion questions, and exercises to search our hearts.

The life of the late Dr. Stephen Olford and his book *The Sword of Suffering* shaped our perspective. As my husband said in the foreword of that book, "As a fellow survivor of cancer, I found that Dr. Stephen Olford has crafted a marvelous text that gives an understanding of God's sovereign grace in the midst of trying circumstances. *The Sword of Suffering* expels the stigma attached with cancer and suffering. It shows how it can be redeemed for the kingdom of God. The investments of the eternal truths continue to make deposits into my daily life."

COMMUNICATION IS CRUCIAL

We were blessed to stay in the Rotary House, next to the M. D. Anderson Cancer Center. I would walk an average of four to six times a day across the bridge connecting the Rotary House and the cancer center. It is a huge hospital, and if it hadn't been for the color-coded departments, we would have been lost more times than we were. The first time we walked through the long corridor, color-coded green, I felt like the actor Michael Clark Duncan in the movie *The Green Mile*. E.K. was about to begin his radiation. In the movie, the long corridor led to death; our hope was that the green corridor stood for life. Day after day we walked that corridor that seemed like a mile.

Soon I realized that not only was I to walk across the bridge from the hospital to the hotel, but I was to be the bridge relaying my husband's condition to his physicians.

Communication is crucial to support the patient. The best place to start—and to return—is as a listener. Initially, I was a listener. As E.K. needed facts, I gave his requests to the doctors. As a spouse, it is very important not to usurp your mate's authority, however. Having cancer did not change my husband's role as the leader of our home, especially when he was able to speak for himself. When you mutually set boundaries while your mate is well, he will be offended if you take certain liberties when he is ill. Communication reduces unnecessary disagreements. There were times I spoke too soon, not giving him the time to speak for himself. Then there were times when I didn't speak fast enough. We also had to deal with our nonverbal communication—especially if one of us was tired, upset, or frustrated.

I learned whenever possible to let my husband lead, especially in conversations. Often E.K. and I realized that people would make contact with me instead of him because he was in a wheelchair. As a result, we had to discuss public communication as well as private communication. A waitress would ask me what he wanted to order when he was able to speak for himself. There were times he would ask a question, and the person whom he asked would attempt to give me the answer.

He would ask, "Why are you giving the answer to my wife? I asked the question."

Bravo for him! Many times we disrespect those who have infirmities because we do not understand their world.

THE FAMILY COMES FIRST

A preacher's son was quoted as saying, "My parents had so much time for everyone else that they didn't have time for me." Sometimes, as a couple, we were guilty of the same indictment. Terminal illness helps you to reprioritize your life and reexamine your core values. Maintaining family unity is a core value. Communication is essential for that to happen.

As parents, we chose to give our two daughters and one son updates of their father's condition before we told others. Our mothers, siblings, extended family, and church leaders were the next persons contacted. Of course, I didn't make all of the calls. One person who knew how to communicate compassionately and correctly would contact another. Eventually there was a list of names of persons who needed to be called, so that coordinator made sure that everyone was contacted. While we lived in Houston, I focused on informing one sibling of each of the Bailey families. That sibling agreed to contact the persons in their family. Talking to them was not a chore. We were as close as sisters and brothers. There was also a list of pastors who were personal friends. I welcomed the time when I was able to share with them on my husband's behalf and return their messages to him. Their expressions of love always uplifted his spirit.

HE IS THE LEADER—SICK OR NOT

My husband's dear friend and Christian brother, Dr. Melvin Wade, who was a leukemia patient prior to my husband's second bout with cancer, counseled us about long-term cancer-patient care. He shared with my husband how his wife's care would seem as though she were mothering him. He told him that my authoritative role was necessary because I would be the one to remind him of the do's and don'ts in order to ensure proper punctual treatment.

After that conversation and others like it, he began to share with me the need for my own rest, especially when E.K. was resting, because it was going to be a tedious journey. Melvin encouraged me to take care of myself because, as my husband, E.K. would not be as comfortable with anyone else as he was with me.

He reminded me of the comfort that I could give that no one else could provide. I soon understood the wisdom of Proverbs 31:11–12: "The heart of her husband trusts in her, . . . She does him good and not evil all the days of her life."

LIVE AT 31 PROVERBS LANE

Once again another model of biblical womanhood was brought to my remembrance. I often refer to Proverbs 31 as living at 31 Proverbs Lane. This is where I needed to reside. My spiritual address has not always been there. There were times that I chose to live at Angry Avenue, Resentment Road, Bitterness Boulevard, and I have even lived at Depressed Drive. Several years ago I was convicted to live at 31 Proverbs Lane before my husband became a cancer patient. My heart's desire is to be a woman, wife, mother, and servant who would glorify God. Therefore, I chose to emulate rather than be intimidated by the woman in the literary photograph.

Despite the challenges or the prognosis, this was not the time for a pity party, nor was it the time to doubt that I was the capable wife who could learn how to be the caregiver for such a time as this. As the mate and a follower of Christ, remember this is a time for biblical affirmation—to meditate and rehearse who you are in Christ.

You are chosen by God.

You are a child of God in His family.

You are sealed with God's Holy Spirit.

You are called to accomplish God's purpose.

You are complete in Christ.

You are being conformed to the character of Christ.

E.K. always made me feel special when he would say, "If I am in a boat that appears to be sinking, I want Sheila to be in that boat." He knew that I had his back as we partnered in ministry. He was the pastor and preacher. I was the Christian Education director for several years. He was the president of E. K. Bailey Ministries; I was the vice president. He was the visionary leader; I was on the implementing team. It was time to go farther in and deeper down, watching God work all things together for our good because we love God and are called according to His purpose (Romans 8:28). His heart was trusting in me to do him "good and not evil all the days of [my] life" (Proverbs 31:12).

With God's help, I could do this four ways. *First, spiritually through daily devotions and prayer.* Usually, I had my devotions before he woke up. Then we had our devotion as a couple while having breakfast. Of course, there were power-point prayers— praying that he would have power from the Holy Spirit to endure the radiation and the chemotherapy. I prayed that he would accept the changes in his body and being away from the family and the church that he loved. There were prayers that the joy of the Lord would be his strength. Prayers were offered unto the Lord every time they would stick him with a needle for blood, especially when his veins were not cooperating due to the chemotherapy. There were prayers that his eyesight would be saved. We needed prayers from one point to another point.

Second, it was vital that both of us stayed as physically fit as we could. His heart was trusting that I would endure during this pilgrimage. Therefore, we needed proper nutrition and rest. During radiation, our sleeping patterns were about normal. When the chemotherapy began, E.K. faced unexpected times of nausea and vomiting. Later there were times of his sleeplessness, uncontrollable itching, and intolerable pain. Sleeping occurred at awkward times. A nap would be taken when we were in the waiting room or the emergency room.

Whenever he took a nap, I tried to nap too. There came the time that he needed around-the-clock care, so someone spent the night with us. I slept in the twin bed next to him with my head at the foot of the bed so he could see me when he was awake. I slept in a lightweight robe because the male caregiver would check on him during the night. Sometimes I slept on the sofa while we were in an apartment while he and the caregiver talked. The caregiver and I alternated sleeping times in order to make sure he had around-the-clock care.

Exercise was important, though the pain in my knees prohibited me from a normal routine of exercise. However, walking daily throughout the hospital from point A to point B gave me the workout that I needed. He needed exercise as well. If he didn't at least walk a certain distance and drink a certain amount of water, he became dehydrated, causing us to go to the emergency room so he could have IVs to give him the proper nourishment. Without a reasonable amount of exercise, some of his body's systems slowed in function. Then there was a need for a feeding tube to be inserted because his throat was too sore to swallow. His appetite fluctuated from normal to only craving certain foods.

Third, mentally we needed to stay sharp. My husband took the thinking process seriously. The author Bob Gass would say he was "intentional about the thinking process." He made thinking a process just as he did prayer, preaching, and family time. Chuck Swindoll would describe him as an eagle type because he aimed high and refused to be bothered by negativism.

E.K. carried many books to Houston. However, fatigue, the side effects of the treatment, and emotional overload sapped the energy from him. There was a void because he couldn't read as he had planned. Yet his heart safely trusted in me to do my best to fill that void. So we talked about the news, magazine articles, and discussions that I'd had. I loved asking him, "What do you think about this?" If I was asking at the wrong time, he would tell me. Otherwise, he had a noteworthy response to any issue. It was wonderful to hear him share his ideas about this book and others, as well as the future plans for the church, anticipating our two daughters and one son being grown. He kept soaring above mediocrity.

Fourth, emotionally his heart trusted in me that I would be a woman who had a calm and quiet spirit (1 Peter 3:3–4). There is an old adage that says, "When Mama is sad, everybody is sad. When Mama is happy, everybody is happy." My modification is, "When Mama or the wife is calm, the house is calm." I didn't need to be a fretting, nagging, worrying woman.

Some days were easier than others, but I had to focus on the Scripture, "Be anxious for nothing, but in everything by prayer and supplication with thanksgiving let your requests be made known to God. And the peace of God, which surpasses all comprehension, will guard your hearts and your minds in Christ Jesus" (Philippians 4:6–7).

It is important that you know your limit and when you need a break. Also you must share with your mate that you are not tired of the work but in the work. Watch for anxiety attacks when the prognosis is discouraging or when you think all of your energy is gone. It's okay to tell your spouse and yourself in a nonlife-threatening moment, "I need time-out."

My "time-out" sometimes was resting on the sofa while he was asleep in the bed. At other times, my time-out was listening to the pianist in one of the waiting areas at M. D. Anderson or listening to a CD on my portable CD player that my sister, Sandra, and my brother-in-law, Rick, gave us. Sometimes it was walking through an undiscovered area of the hospital while he was in a treatment or meeting a new person. Sometimes it was being still and praising God for His provision or beholding the beauty of His creation as I looked out of the window or sat in the courtyard.

I even had to ask God for discernment regarding his anxieties. The spouse is always an encourager either by words, by deeds, or by nonverbal communication. You must seek to find the balance between saying you can do more and "Let's wait and try again." Accepting your mate's changing condition is very important to his self-acceptance during this time. Reading the information about possible side effects increases your awareness, but there is an emotional adjustment when you wake up and see locks of hair on the pillow for the first time. When your spouse looks in your eyes to see whether your eyes still accept and love him, it is so important that your verbal and nonverbal language communicates that.

CELEBRATE THE LANDMARKS

E.K. has mentioned how every patient needs to celebrate. Yes, celebrate the progress and the achievements of the patient. Our daughter Shenikwa, who is an elementary school teacher, bought poster board, paper, and labels and then added those affirming messages—"Good Job" and "Outstanding" to "Super"—after learning Dad wanted a visual reminder that the number of treatments was decreasing. She designed this special calendar for the eight weeks of radiation. Every day he would see me place a label on that calendar. It was visually encouraging—a daily celebration and a countdown to the final treatment.

One week before the final treatment, the church was making plans to witness him ringing the bell. When I was informed that over one hundred people were planning to attend, I knew that could bring havoc to the hospital's organization, as well as upset other patients. I started wearing the hat of an event planner by contacting the patient director, who in conjunction with our church liaison, Pastor Rod Stodgill, facilitated this in an orderly fashion. Two highlights from that day: Our children wore the special T-shirts that read "Daddy, You Did It!" with a bell in the center. And the men of our church's staff had their heads shaved to convey the message that, "Pastor, we identify with you. You are not by yourself."

E.K. and I celebrated the medical staff by providing beautiful angels to the doctors and the key administrative support staff. God gave us favor through them, and I will always be their ardent fan. A celebration second to none, orchestrated by Dr. Wright Lassiter, Associate Pastor of Development, was held at our church in November. It began a national campaign to encourage and support a man who many people proclaimed as a preacher-pastor extraordinaire, who labored in the service of the Lord. The Concord Baptist Church led the way, showing how to love their pastor and his family, followed by countless numbers of pastors and friends throughout the metroplex and country. Dr. C. B. T. Smith, who had been his pastor for many years, preached the celebratory sermon.

The family continued to celebrate our family's birthdays, and on our thirty-fourth wedding anniversary, Dr. Smith asked Rick Jordan to coordinate a surprise anniversary dinner for us. It was a culinary delight, prepared by a young caterer, Fitzgerald Dodd. In September 2003, there was another "Celebrate the Recovery" campaign, coordinated by Melba Smith, who gave the celebratory message. You may ask, "Why the celebration when it looks like he is getting weaker?" We continued to celebrate life and the belief that God would heal him on earth or in heaven. "For the Lord God is a sun and shield; the Lord gives grace and glory; no good thing does He withhold from those who walk uprightly" (Psalm 84:11).

NO GREATER LOVE: A CAREGIVER

Later, after final appointments in Houston, we again saw the power and comfort of having a caregiver and helpers. It was time to pack the belongings at our temporary home of Rotary House. Melba Smith, who with Rick Jordan and Hansel Cunningham had packed, drove, and moved us into the Rotary House, said, "I took Pastor to Houston. I'm bringing him home."

The night before our scheduled departure, my husband became so ill that we had to take him to the emergency room. Melba said, "I'm not leaving until he is well enough to take the trip." As we approached Dallas, cell phones were ringing inquiring about our location. Their father, son, brother, brother-in-law, uncle, pastor, and neighbor was returning, and they were waiting to welcome him. It was phenomenal to see how a church community and country celebrated the victory through the battle.

Our house manager, Mrs. Dixie Daughtry, made sure that the house would pass a white-glove inspection. Vents had been cleaned, air purifiers had been purchased, and the carpet had been shampooed in anticipation of his arrival. The time came that Pastor Bailey led the church in celebrating Hansel Cunningham, an elder of our church who became the pastor's caregiver. Hansel committed to take us to every doctor's appointment in Dallas, out of the city, and even out of the country. He also tailor-made his schedule to accommodate all of his pastor's needs. No greater love had we seen demonstrated. With love, strength, dignity, and dependability, he was there, assisted by Bro. Felix Spencer. We will always be indebted to him and his wife, Lillian, for their loving commitment.

ALTERNATIVE TREATMENTS

What do you do when the doctors say, "I'm sorry that there isn't a treatment or a drug we can give you"? You keep searching for new possibilities. We were introduced to alternative medicine by cancer survivors. Our eyes were opened to a discipline of which we had very little knowledge.

I highly recommend *An Alternative Medicine: Definitive Guide to Cancer* by W. John Diamond, M.D., and W. Lee Cowden, M.D., with Burton Goldberg. The authors note that new studies and polls indicate a steadily rising acceptance of alternative medicine as a treatment option for disease. More alternative practices are being included in cancer care, they write. This resource has served as a guide to give us a panoramic view for treating cancer and knowing the politics of cancer.

We began to search for alternative treatments in the United States, as well as in Vancouver, British Columbia. A physician would ask questions on our behalf to ensure the qualifications of those we were consulting for treatment. During this time, the Reverend McKinley Hailey introduced us to Malcolm Hoarde, who changed our dietary habits. Malcolm Hoarde has a passion for nutritional healing. Every day, often more than once, he brought vegetarian meals to our house. He is a walking encyclopedia in the area of nutritional healing.

This was a new discipline for my husband. He tried more and more of their foods. He gave me the freedom to choose as well. I enjoyed many of the foods that I tasted. The vegetarian pizza, lasagna, and the wheat pancakes were my favorites. Another book, *Prescription for Nutritional Healing* by Phyllis A. Balch and James. F. Balch, is an excellent resource as you seek to have a better understanding of the elements of health disorders and therapies.

It has been said that most of us eat for taste, cost, and convenience. Dr. Richard J. Stephenson, a pioneer in comprehensive cancer treatment, believes that, "A well-nourished cancer patient can better manage and beat the disease."

IT'S THE PATIENT'S CHOICE— IF YOUR INSURANCE SAYS "NO"

It would have been easier if we would have seen the article in 2001 when the insurance company said "No" to our request to receive treatment out of network. It is apparent that God still works miracles, gives wisdom and discernment, and places people in strategic areas when you have no one but Him to call and depend on. Do yourself a favor and read the *Parade* magazine article "Treatment—Tailor Made for You," published September 19, 2004, and available on the Internet at (http://archive.parade.com/2004/0919/0919/_treatment-tailor.html). It gives the importance of personalized medical care based upon your family history. This article tells you how to develop a personalized health plan, assess your health risks, and research prescription drugs.

Perhaps you are saying, "I'm not Pastor Bailey. My insurance won't pay. What news do you have for us?" E.K. would say, "I'm glad you asked," because the same issue of *Parade* published a practical article entitled "When Your Insurance Won't Pay," written by Dr. Jason Theodosakis and David T. Feinberg and reproduced at the *Parade* magazine Web site (http://archive.parade.com/2004/0919/0919/_insurance.html). It offers these tips:

- Don't get angry but do get involved.

- Hold on to your written records.

- Talk to your doctor about the reason for the denial (drug or treatment).

- Realize that most plans base coverage on a concept called "medically necessary."

- Do research.

- Contact your insurance company and say, "I am appealing my denied care." This puts it in writing. Also, with many long-term health policies, there is a one-hundred-day deductible. Please read your policy. Start counting your one hundred days so that you can receive the benefit of what you have been investing.

• Notify your department of human resources at work. Your company's head of personnel or human resources may get involved, putting proper pressure on the insurance company they have contracted with for their employees' welfare.

• Finally, if you think a treatment or medication is urgent or required, get it.

These writers express the sentiments of our family when they say, "Don't be afraid to go to bat against your insurance company and turn its *no* into a healthy *yes*."

Finally, *pray*. Discuss the health-care options with the patient but agree that it is the patient's choice. Pray together for wisdom in making the right decisions.

DEVELOP A WINNING TEAM

So much work needs to be done that one caregiver can't do it all. The more visible the spouse, the wider the network. Although our primary focus is the patient, other people can help you maintain a degree of normalcy in an abnormal situation.

Assess your needs outside of patient care. Mandatory items, such as doctors' appointments, bills to be paid, bank deposits, and other chores, can be time-consuming and deny quality time with the patient and your children. You can't enjoy that time when you are frantic and frazzled. Needs will change depending upon the stage of the illness. What can be delegated: sorting the mail, logging the mail, ordering medicine, picking up the medicine, giving updates, answering the phone, and buying groceries. Determine who will perform these tasks. Pray. Some will volunteer, but it must be people who will help you to accomplish the tasks, and not provide an admission ticket to visit him.

Our team went far beyond our primary caregiver, Hansel Cunningham, and our big-hearted helper, Melba Smith. Some practical ways people served us were:

- They accompanied us to the doctor.

- They gave the gift of humor, including videos of the Three Stooges and Mickey Mouse.

- They brought not only food to the family but also inquired about our preferences. Two of the three children have allergies. I appreciated their discernment.

- They brought good times to us. Due to his condition, I wasn't able to go to the State Fair of Texas. He and I always love to partake of all of the delicacies. Therefore, loved ones brought the family smoked turkey legs. Deeelicious!

- They remembered the overlooked items, e.g., an e-mail station or pleasant games. Since I wasn't computer literate, a friend purchased an e-mail station and also taught me how to use it. Some gave word search books. I had a goodie bag for the two of us, and in later stages, there was a goodie bag for each one of us.

- They gave practical gifts. They treated me to beauty-shop appointments and offered assistance in easy-care styles. There were gift certificates of every sort: certificates for the grocery store, massage parlor, hair salon, nail salon, restaurants, movies, videos, and DVDs. Some just gave us cash to use as we needed. Friends delivered cases of water. Every ministry in our church showed us love and kindness, with gifts ranging from complimentary dinners to originally designed cards that showcased the talents and love of the children and youth ministries.

• The Baptist Ministers Union, under the leadership of Dr. S. J. Gilbert, extended every courtesy in a generous manner to our family, not only during the time that we resided in Houston for the treatments, but upon our return to Dallas. Thus the annual International Expository Preaching Conference developed by E. K. Bailey Ministries (a nonprofit ministry with a mission to impart the Word of God to church leaders and promote a biblically healthy church) continued to be inspirational and informative. The church continued to grow, souls were saved, and ministries continued to labor diligently, equipping the saints for ministry. The quality of preaching was never compromised. Some of the best national pulpiteers also preached during his illness.

Our children were a vital part of this time. They were added as cosigners to our bank accounts. Before we could arrange for automatic drafts, Shenikwa and I discussed what bills needed to be paid, and she paid them. Our oldest daughter, Cokiesha, worked at the church in the senior pastor's (her dad's) office. She became the public relations liaison. She knew what, when, and how to articulate his and our families' condition. Two of my sisters-in-law were also on the team, Dorothy Bailey and Vivian Flakes.

MAKE THE SACRIFICE

So many people have asked me, "What was it like to go through cancer with your husband?" "What comfort would you forsake?" "What career opportunity would you decline for the life of your husband?" There was nothing too important for me to forsake in order to help save my husband's life. I vowed " . . . for better or for worse."

There is an old classic hymn with the lyrics, "Jesus paid it all. All to Him I owe." When I think about what Jesus did for me through E. K. Bailey for more than thirty years, whatever I could do, however I could care, whatever expressions of love could be made, it was my heart's desire to do so. When your loved one's life is at risk, what is it that you won't do for that person?

I hope you answered, "Nothing." It's easy to say that. The test comes when it is ninety degrees in Texas and your patient has cold intolerance. A low fan becomes too cold, and all vents have to be sealed in your bedroom and bathroom. The two of you want to spend time together, but you feel like you are going to pass out. It takes much prayer, communication, and flexibility.

What are you willing to clean? Caregiving means cleaning the vomit, giving suppositories, cleaning the bedpan, changing the bed pads and sheets at any time, helping the patient in and out of the shower, bathing the patient in bed, and lifting the patient off the commode. You are doing the work that a nurse, patient assistant, technician, or a hospital floor supervisor would perform, while you love him as a wife. You must also keep the patient looking good.

BE ALERT TO CHANGING NEEDS

There were many stages during which he was very functional in spite of discomfort. During those times we would go to the movies or dine out at a restaurant. When doctors in Atlanta, Georgia, and Vancouver, British Columbia, were seeing him, we would see the beauty of those cities. One day he told Hansel Cunningham while we were in Vancouver, "Show me some of the sights." He found a restaurant in an area that was indescribably beautiful. It overlooked a pier surrounded by mountains, through which a train coursed. To be there enjoying each other and God's creation of nature in another country was a cherished moment.

Later, when his health changed, the beauty was appreciated from the patio. The stages kept changing. The beauty was seen from the corner room of the seventh floor of Methodist Hospital, as we viewed the spectacular skyline of downtown Dallas. The final view was down in the bedroom. In a bedroom that had been our daughters', he could see the travelers go by while the squirrels climbed the tree in front of the window.

With each stage there were different needs. Continuously take inventory of what equipment, supplies, and clothes are needed. These were a few items that we needed: hearing aids, oxygen, oximeter, socks that were very soft and stretchable, a cushion for the wheelchair, a pen that is easy for a patient who has neuropathy to use, a spittoon, a pillow for his back, and slippers that would look good when worn with a suit.

This all seems like tough work, and many times it is. But it's all part of bringing your behavior in line with your beliefs, something I heard emphasized as a young woman pursuing a Christian Education degree at Bishop College in Dallas. The lesson lasted. It's a principle Jesus taught and one E.K. would say is part of moving farther in and deeper down with our Lord.

HEART NOTES
FROM THE FAMILY

THE SON SHINES ON RAINY DAYS

Whenever the soloist sang "Precious Memories—How They Linger" in my home church, Faith Tabernacle Baptist Church in Stamford, Connecticut, those who recently had experienced the death of a loved one became quite emotional. I didn't grasp how the song seemed to pick at your emotional scar until my parents and husband died. Now the sweet memories have such a bitter, lingering effect, causing bottomless pain.

It doesn't seem so long ago that I met E. K. Bailey. It was on September 15, 1965, in the dining hall at Bishop College in Dallas, Texas. Precious memories, how they linger:

- Four years of dating during college
- The first date to church

- The walks in the rain on the college campus

- Eating together on the public side of the dining hall after a church had given him a "love" offering for preaching versus eating on the side with a student prepaid meal ticket. There was quite a difference.

- Taking classes together

- Doing homework together

- Graduating from college in 1969

- Being married that August at St. John Baptist Church, Oklahoma City, where his godfather, Rev. Dr. W. K. Jackson, pastored and performed the ceremony.

- Living in our first apartment in Fort Worth, while he was a student at Southwestern Baptist Theological Seminary

- Accepting his first pastorate, Mt. Carmel Baptist Church, Dallas (December 1969)

- Founding Concord Missionary Baptist Church in Dallas (June 1975)

- Sharing in the births of our children, Cokiesha, Shenikwa, and Emon

- Founding E. K. Bailey Ministries

- Becoming an author while he was a cancer patient. Even now his voice is heard from heaven.

- Recalling memories of his favorite delectable cuisine, his warm embraces, robust laughter, honest transparency, bulldog tenacity, visionary leadership, caring, great preaching, and, of course, being a loving father and my husband

E.K. was a trailblazer in many aspects of the growth and development in the African-American church. "This has never been done before," he said. However, it wasn't an excuse for E.K. to use if God was leading him. He was my pal, prophet, priest, partner, and protector. He was the man who loved, critiqued, and coached me to be all God wanted me to be.

God's love permeated through him to exhort me to be equipped for the future as he encouraged me to:

- Go inside the bank and not just to the drive-thru windows: "The people need to know you too."

- Do my best: "That's not your best! Start over. That's better; I knew you could do it!"

- Complete the task: "Do what it takes, if it means getting started at 3 a.m."

- Have fun: "You need some serendipitous moments. Have fun—laugh!"

- Give God a rested and ready body. "Before you teach— let God simmer the message through the Holy Spirit in your mind and heart."

- Know that failure isn't final.

The memories aren't as savory as milk chocolate. They can be likened to bittersweet chocolate. I know that day by day the sweetness of the memories will eventually linger more than the pain.

As I glanced out of the window today, I sensed that there was an overcast in more ways than one, but hours later the sun shone through the clouds. Every day, by faith, I choose not to focus on the overcast but on the *Son* who is shining. As He shines, those *Son* rays replace the clouds of anxiety, fear, worry, and loneliness. To focus on Psalm 23:6 brings hope and joy to the believer's heart: "I will dwell in the house of the Lord forever."

That is where he is now!

My heart longs to paint a picture of our pilgrimage. It would replicate a scene that occurs in Dallas where it is raining while the sun is shining. I would use bright colors depicting the vibrancy of my husband's personality, preaching, and pastoring. These would be blended with the subdued colors of uncertainty. Painted on the canvas would be the soft pastels representing the peace and tranquility that God gave us.

The picture would portray a middle-aged father and mother with two young adult daughters working in the city and a young adult son entering Lon Morris College in Jacksonville, Texas, as a freshman. The picture would be like a kaleidoscope, because the scenes would change from work to home, church, and fun times. The cities would change from Dallas to Houston to Atlanta, Georgia, and to Vancouver, British Columbia—the cities where he had had treatments.

Sonshine always intrudes on the rain. One day, with the nasopharyngeal cancer in remission, doctors saw tiny nodules, too small to biopsy, in his lungs. What were they? Finally, it was confirmed that the cancer had metastasized to the lungs. We knew that God had the final say on his length of time, but we asked, "What is the prognosis?" It could have been as soon as six months. It was the most difficult day for us. The sky seemed dark. There was always the possibility that our circumstances were going to worsen, but by faith we kept praying, hoping, and striving for healing. Often my husband would say, "Face what's facing you." We needed time and a place to bounce back.

From the doctor's appointment, we went to Joe Pool Lake. The three of us were in the car, E.K., Hansel Cunningham, and me. Silence filled the air. There were conversations, but not audible. Each one of us was petitioning God to have mercy, and to give us wisdom and strength. God energized us for what was to follow.

We called for our children, mother, siblings, and extended family to come to the house. In a very short period of time, we were all there. They anticipated the reason we were together. There was an array of emotions from "It couldn't be" . . . "What a shame" . . . "It is not. I will not receive it," to an outburst of anger: "How can God do this?"

Now E.K. made sure the Son shined on this sad scene. The preacher, pastor, husband, father, and man of God began to counsel us, assuring us that as believers we have the promises, presence, and power of God.

As we prayed, God began comforting us for what was ahead. On those kinds of days, our adult daughters received consolation by getting in bed with their daddy, and our son by being by his bedside.

In our final days together, E.K. and I shared a deep intimacy. As beautiful and invigorating as sex is in a marriage, intimacy has a longer endurance. Do yourself a favor and read the book of Solomon. He and the Shulamite love of his life had a multisensory intimacy. That kind of intimacy gives continual fulfillment in all areas. Don't allow cancer or any terminal illness to become a barrier to intimacy. Don't cave in to the thinking that you can't survive without sexual intercourse in marriage during critical health.

Identify the barriers to intimacy, which can include, as author Shirley E. Montgomery writes in *Winning Ways for Ministers Wives*, self-centeredness, fear of being hurt, unresolved conflict, emotional hang-ups, poor communication, and lack of caring. Creatively your marriage can flourish, so both of you can remain true to your marriage vows through sickness and health and for better or for worse.

Talk about what satisfies each other, especially during this season of life. E.K. and I had often prayed that busyness would not be a hindrance to our marriage. During the times of illness, God multiplied the quality of intimacy.

Two days before he died, he asked me to get in the bed—a hospital bed—with him. He wasn't able to move his body, but his mind and emotions were intact. Vivian, his sister, moved him over. When I was in the bed, most of me was hanging out. Shenikwa, my daughter, lifted the railing so I wouldn't fall out. It was a beautiful time of intimacy. It endures to the end.

SHEILA M. BAILEY

THOSE COWBOYS
KNOW HOW TO DIE

When we gathered together as a family in order to have a good time, movie watching always seemed to play a special part of that time. My mother and sister would prefer action-packed movies and animated movies. I always preferred romantic love stories and historical films. My brother enjoyed suspense movies and comedies.

My father, on the other hand, enjoyed all of the above. He was certainly a movie buff. He watched various films, digested them, and then redigested them. He always found a way to turn them into sermon illustrations.

Most people do not know that my father was very fond of westerns. He watched some of the best actors and actresses fight it out on the big screen. He would sit up in the bed and root for John Wayne, Ward Bond, Henry Brandon, Olive Carey, Jeffrey Hunter, and others as they exhausted themselves in some of the best westerns ever made. I can still remember my dad watching TV, on several occasions, with such intensity that one would wonder if he knew the actors personally. He became so engaged and even submerged himself into the story as the plot thickened.

One day, I watched a few of the westerns with him, and I found myself yawning, nodding, and desperately hoping that we could turn to something that would interest us both. He would say, "Okay, Kiesha, I'll change the channel, but I have to see one thing . . ."

Then, like clockwork, he would sit up as straight as possible with his eyes glued to the TV. He would grab his pillow as though it were trying to run away from him. He would stare at the screen with the attention that most of us give an urgent weather report.

I would just sit back and watch him as he became the personal cheerleader and number-one fan of the cast members. Daddy would look at the screen and cheer, "Yeah!!!" He would fall back into the bed and roll around the bed laughing. He would look back at the screen and cheer again, "That's right! Get 'em! Go after it, boy!" Sometimes he would stand up and walk up to the television as though the actors could hear him. He would start fanning the TV. He would say, "That's it! That's it! You're doing it!"

I got such a kick out of Daddy's humorous expression of love for these films. It seemed like it became a pastime of his. It relaxed him, made him laugh, took his mind off his illness, and of course, gave him preaching illustrations.

At first I couldn't understand his passion for westerns. One day I asked him, "Daddy, what in the world do you get out of watching those boring westerns?"

"Those cowboys sure know how to die," he answered.

I looked puzzled, and he continued. "You see, when they are gunned down by another cowboy, they don't go down easily. They roll to the left, and then they roll to the right. They stagger a while. They may hit the ground a couple of times. They might bang their heads against a water trough; they might roll around in the dust and crawl up the steps to the parlor, but they keep fighting. They don't quit. They don't give up easily."

As I watched my dad approach his last days, I remembered those special times when we watched westerns as a family. I remembered the look on his face as he watched the cowboys fight. I recalled the fun he had, the sounds he made, and the things that he said as he watched what he considered to be some of the best films ever made. I still couldn't get over how much he enjoyed watching the fighting of the cowboys, but even more so, I remembered how he became so excited by the way the cowboys died.

As I watched my dad prepare for his transition from this life to his eternal home, I found so many similarities between my father's death and the death of those heroic cowboys. Just as he had developed a fondness for western films, I was developing a fondness for watching God at work in Daddy's final hours.

In the past, death had been a word that I didn't like. I didn't want to talk about death, I didn't want to think about death, and, most of all, I didn't want to even consider the fact that my parents would one day pass away. Death always seemed so final to me. It always made me feel robbed. When I experienced the loss of my godbrother, A.B., when I was in college and even the loss of cousins, schoolmates, mentors, and grandparents, I found myself feeling sad, abandoned, and alone.

I wrestled with the fact that God loves us, yet allows us to experience such traumatic pain when losing someone special. I felt like I was going through life blindfolded, trying to feel my way through without them.

Later, as I witnessed my father in his last days, God re-created a totally new image for me about death. The Lord allowed me to see that the death of His saints is really beautiful. It is a mysterious process, where God prepares our character for our heavenly home.

When the nurses came in to tell us that he was dying, we were stunned because he was still alert and speaking clearly. We thought a person who was dying would be in a comatose state. We struggled with the fact that the report was not good, but he looked well and had no problem sharing with us what was on his mind. Even when he became too weak to speak, we would ask him questions, and he would nod. He mustered up enough energy during those final five days to give us instructions and to encourage us. That didn't seem like a man who was dying.

One day we asked him what he wanted to watch on television, and he said baseball. He loved baseball, and he watched it there in the hospital attentively. We asked if we could sing to him and pray for him, and he consented. He even closed his eyes and smiled as we were singing some of his favorite songs. He drank juices, allowed my aunt to massage him, and talked to me about school.

One day he looked at me and asked, "When are you going back to school?" I didn't want to tell him that the doctors asked me to hang around because they believed that he was going to die any day. Therefore, I asked, "Well, when do you think I should go back to school?"

He looked at me and in a clear voice said, "Tomorrow."

"But I don't want to leave you."

He continued by saying, "Kiesha, I have taught you how to swim. Now just do it."

I was amazed. That didn't sound like someone who was dying.

He then asked my mother to get in the bed with him. He would hold her and kiss her and snuggle. He would ask for my sister and brother to come close to the bed so that he could tell them something or joke or kiss them. He would look at me and smile and wait for me to kiss him on the forehead and smile again.

When the nurses would come in, he would tell them that he was ready to go home. They would encourage him to just get comfortable there in the hospital bed, and he would tell them that he couldn't be comfortable until he was home in his own bed. He appeared to be our "regular daddy." He was still funny, charming, and taking charge. How could he really be dying? He was mentally alert and everything.

He then requested that we schedule a time for his African friend and "son in the ministry," Rev. Isaac Soda, to come and visit him. He seemed adamant about meeting with him. Reverend Soda arrived, and right there in the hospital my dad conducted a meeting regarding Pastor Soda's return to Africa. He wanted to see how our church could assist him and his family in returning home. He also wanted to talk about how we could meet the needs of our brothers and sisters in the motherland. This was really something. How could he be dying? He had just planned and conducted a meeting.

The nurses then asked us to go in and say our good-byes to him. That felt strange, because he seemed to have life and living at the forefront of his mind. However, we honored their request. We told him how much we loved him and thanked him for providing for us. We shared with him all of the special memories that we had. We even recalled areas where we needed to ask for his forgiveness. It was clearly a "come to Jesus" kind of meeting.

He did the same with us. He shared his heart, affirmed each of us with his words, and pretty much told us good-bye.

The nurses asked him to try to get some rest. He told them that he wouldn't go to sleep until he got home. Even after we pleaded with him to sleep, we watched him stay awake for three solid days. It was unbelievable. Each of us took turns falling asleep, and when every one of us woke up, he was looking at us. It really was astonishing.

One night he asked me if I could see what he saw. He pointed up to the sky and smiled. I told him that I couldn't see it. He looked at me in disbelief because he really seemed to have wanted me to see what he was seeing. He then told us that he wanted all of us to get on "a train with him." We said okay, trying to follow along, not knowing if he was hallucinating because of the medicine. Then, he looked at each of us, smiled, and sighed with a sense of relief that we were all together.

Then he said, "No, you all can't go on this train ride. Just me."

We were frozen. We stood there not knowing how to respond.

Another time he looked up again and said, "E. K. Bailey is out of here." It seemed that he was keenly aware of what was happening to him. He told us several times that we were going to be fine, and he asked us to take care of our mother. He told us that he was proud of us and to work hard. He even said, "Lift up the name of Jesus."

It occurred to me that my dad was fighting just like those cowboys that he once cheered for. Cancer had crept into his body several years ago in his kidney, and he had surgery. God healed him, and he went to work again as a soldier in God's great army. Then, years later, cancer returned in his nasal passage. He received several treatments, which caused him to have to pastor his church differently. He had to learn how to preach differently. He had to walk and talk and eat differently, but he kept living. He began to write books and more books. He began to teach passionately on the causes, effects, and preventative methods of cancer. He preached a marriage series at our church. For most of the sermons, he was seated. When he wanted to stand, he was assisted by a cane, but he kept preaching.

Now, here on his deathbed, he kept instructing, advising, caring, and loving. Like the cowboys, he was determined to not go down easily.

It blessed me to see my father battle cancer so courageously three times. It really made me feel honored to have a father who was so generous and caring that he would make provisions for his family. He revealed his passion for God's church and his selflessness when he asked our church to appoint his assistant pastor as his successor in the event that he passed away. It watered our souls to hear him tell us again and again how much he loved us.

Daddy had become the cowboy whom he used to root for on the screen. He didn't go down without a fight. Daddy captured us by the way he lived and by the way he died. What a hero!

I praise God for my father's godly example. I will always remember his quick wit and hearty laugh. I will be forever grateful for his intentionality in living a holy life. I will continue to marvel at his preaching gifts and his passion for preparing preachers to impart the Word. But what I appreciate the most is his introducing my siblings and me to Christ. Now, we have accepted the challenge of "living and dying well."

Death is no longer a dirty word to me. It is one that makes me look forward to joining the cloud of witnesses. It represents to me a comma, a brief separation. I am so happy that I didn't say good-bye to my father forever. I am sure, because of my hope in Jesus, that I will see him again.

Death and *dying* have become words that make me smile . . . because God is there.

I am not consumed by my father's absence because my other father, my Everlasting Father, will never die, and we shall reign with Him one day. My heart leaps as I consider God's faithfulness. When we are sick, He is faithful. When we are well, He is faithful. When we are at our best, He is faithful; and when we have reached our lowest point, He is faithful.

God never leaves us. He carries us. He comforts us. He corrects us. He cheers for us, and He captures us by His faithfulness to us.

God colors our world with His character. He takes the blues and burgundies, pinks and reds, grays and blacks, gold and beige colors of life, and He blends them until the picture becomes something magnificent. He takes our lives like a painter takes a bare canvas, and He splashes colors together until He has designed an attractive and exquisite masterpiece. The process is tedious, but the product is timeless.

Even in the midst of suffering and sorrow, we can see His brilliant signature all around us.

COKIESHA L. BAILEY

SEEING GOD'S
STRENGTH, POWER, AND GRACE

I couldn't think, sleep, or concentrate. I became difficult to be around. I was depressed, confused and, above all, *angry*. It wasn't enough that every day for the past two years, I've had to watch my daddy physically decline. It wasn't enough that the man who had been the rock of our family had lost his ability to walk without assistance. Now, to learn that I have health issues.

Am I committing a sin to be *angry* with God? Am I wrong to feel like God has completely forsaken me? What happened to Joshua 1:5, "I will never leave you nor forsake you"? What about 1 Corinthians 10:13, "I won't put more on you than you can bear"? For the first time in my life, I felt as if God did not hold to His end of the bargain. I was depressed, confused and, above all, *angry*.

Five years earlier, in the fall of 1997, while attending Clark Atlanta University, I received a phone call that rocked my world. My mother called and told me that my daddy's doctor found a mass on his kidney. She said the doctor wanted to operate. "When the surgery is scheduled, I will arrange for you to come home," my mother said. I got off the phone and was very confused. Maybe it was denial, but I didn't know that my mom was talking about cancer! After talking with my roommate, Tiffany, I knew I should call my mom back for clarification. I honestly did not want to call back. I wanted to believe that it was nothing. I could not begin to think that something could possibly be wrong with *my daddy!!*

When I called back I flat out asked my mother, "Is this mass CANCER?" She responded, "Yes." I really do not remember how we got off the telephone or how I made it back to my bedroom. What I do remember is lying flat on the floor and crying and praying uncontrollably. That day was the beginning of my new prayer life. Never before had I cried out to God. Never before had I begged Him on behalf of anyone but myself. Never before had I so desperately needed God to show His supernatural power than at that very moment. Daddy had surgery, we moved into our new church building, everything was going well and I was fine.

Then in August 2001, I was in a staff development meeting when I saw our home number flash on my cell phone screen. I excused myself and accepted the call. I had been anxiously awaiting the report of my daddy's biopsy. My mom's overly cheerful tone gave it away. I listened as she explained the tumor was cancerous. I asked her how daddy was doing, and she said, "You know your father."

At the end of the day I reluctantly went home. I knocked on my parent's bedroom door. My father was lying down. I crawled into my daddy's big ol' arms, and I cried and prayed. Shortly after, Mamma and Daddy temporarily moved to Houston for chemo and radiation at M.D. Anderson. Eventually the cancer was gone, and I was fine.

But the next summer I faced another day of anticipating the results of still another biopsy. This time I did not feel hopeful for Daddy—this was the heaviest day of my life. It wasn't that I doubted God; it was almost like He was preparing me for the devastating news we were about to receive. The family gathered yet again at our home and awaited my parents' arrival from the doctor's office.

After Mamma and Daddy were home, they sat on one couch. Kiesha, Emon, and I sat on the opposite couch. The rest of the family just stood around the living room.

Daddy started speaking in his normal slow, deep voice. He got straight to the point and said, "The cancer has metastasized to my lungs." I felt my heart drop to my stomach. He went on to say, "This type of cancer cannot be treated with chemo nor radiation nor an operation." I was sure that I was not breathing. I felt dizzy and queasy, but Daddy was not finished. He continued with, "And the doctor has given me six months to a year to live."

That was it. I lost it. I started gasping for air and crying. The next thirty minutes seemed like a blur. A couple family members began to cry; most of the family seemed to be frozen with shock. My mother cried as she sat next to my daddy and ever so gently rubbed his back. An aunt and uncle started praying and singing praise songs. One family member literally vomited. To sum it all up, it was pure pandemonium.

When everyone seemed to have gotten it together, Daddy's voice rang out like a bell in the middle of the night. He said, "Now this is the next step." He ended his talk with this, "I am not a quitter, and I won't quit now." The next step was to research alternative medicines and procedures. We did exactly that. Daddy started receiving treatments and changed his diet to a vegetarian regimen (except for those rare times when he just had to have some chicken or lemon-pepper wings).

My daddy had cancer. I knew that. Cancer could take his life. I understood that. So everything was okay and I was fine! I really did feel fine. I didn't feel sick or anything, so what is going on? My hair is shedding! Day by day, I would have a comb full of hair every time I ran it through to my scalp.

Catherine, my hair stylist, could see what I couldn't see. She saw the quarter size bald spot grow to a bald spot the size of the palm of my hand. She suggested that I make an appointment with my dermatologist. On the day of my appointment, Catherine accompanied me.

The doctor asked if I were under any stress. I said, "Well, I'm an elementary school teacher, a twenty-six year old balancing all of the responsibilities that come along with that (whatever they are). I live a fast-paced life (but who doesn't), and, by the way, my daddy is a cancer patient." He asked me how I was dealing with that. I said (you guessed it) "I'm fine!" He prescribed an ointment and foam treatment to be applied. My hairstylist and I applied it. I started a year-long routine of cortisone injections into my scalp.

As we were exiting the exam room, the doctor said to me, "Miss Bailey, you really need to try to alleviate some of the stress in your life." "Easy for you to say, Mr. Doctor," I thought. "Do you have to watch your daddy suffer day in and day out fighting his third bout with cancer? Most importantly, don't tell me to alleviate stress when every single strand of hair is falling out of my head, and you can't tell me why!"

Eventually, that is exactly what happened. Every single strand of hair fell out of my head. Actually, every strand of hair on my body fell out. All I knew was that I had alopecia. No one could offer a cause or a cure. I can't begin to explain the depression, the confusion and, above all, the anger. I can honestly say that I never had major self-esteem issues. My parents did a great job instilling in me Christ-esteem. I suffered from eczema as a child and eventually outgrew it, for the most part. That was the extent of any physical problems I faced. Sure, I wished I were a few pounds lighter, a little taller and maybe had clearer skin, but, for the most part, I didn't have issues with my appearance. I was comfortable with Shenikwa.

Now at twenty-six, I have become so self absorbed and so paranoid about my looks. It was a shock to me. I didn't like the person I had become—looking in the mirror every ten minutes, asking people how I looked and obsessing over the smallest things. I felt like the loss of my hair robbed me of who I was. I felt like wearing a wig made me someone else and hindered me from being myself.

I am an energetic fifth grade teacher who enjoys interacting with my students. It would not be out of the norm to see me running around outside, turning flips or just having a good ol' laugh with my students. Now I'm not that same teacher. I can't be as free with them as I once was because everything was about my hair loss and my new best friend—the WIG!

One day at school my worst nightmare almost came true. I was walking down the stairs with the other two fifth grade teachers. We were laughing and having a good time. I was laughing so hard that I lost my balance and fell down the last two steps. (Go ahead and laugh.) Anyway, I hit my knee really hard. I grabbed my knee and slung my head back grimacing with pain. Before I knew it, my wig slid back about five inches. The pain in my knee prevented me from realizing what was happening. One of the teachers ran to my side and started fixing the wig.

I praised the Lord for two things at that moment. First, that none of my students was around, and secondly, that I had already shared with those two teachers about my hair situation. I then went into the teachers' lounge and called my boyfriend of ten years, searching for some encouragement. He asked me if I were all right and if the students were around. He then told me everything was going to be okay and try to calm down. He assured me of his love for me and told me to call him back if I needed to. I locked myself in the bathroom and cried like a baby.

If I've learned nothing else during this wintry season, I have learned that stress is real. Stress can take a toll on your body, mind, and spirit, especially during the time of suffering and death. According to the World English Dictionary, "Stress is mental, emotional, or physical strain, caused, for example, by anxiety or overwork. It may cause such symptoms as raised blood pressure or depression."

At no point in time did I ever feel overwhelmed with the stress during the course of this cancer journey with my daddy and even with the loss of my hair. At times I felt sad. I even cried. At other times I felt worried, so I prayed. There were even times when I felt hope, so I rejoiced. I honestly thought I was coping well with these issues.

It wasn't until later that I would find out that all I was doing was internalizing my true feelings. I never verbally shared with anyone that I was scared to death. I never acknowledged the fact that cancer was slowly eating away the very life of my daddy, and I honestly felt scared and helpless.

People would ask how I was doing, and, with sincerity, I would respond, " I'm fine" or " Just pray for us." Those were responses that I could say and not start crying. Everything became about not crying. Why? Who teaches us that crying is a sign of weakness? Where do we learn to cope instead of cry? What's wrong with a good cry every now and then? Who was going to fault me for an uncontrollable cry for the man I've loved since birth? Surely, a few tears could have been shed for my dearest friend, my distinguished pastor, and my dedicated supporter, my DADDY!

Steve, now my husband, would constantly encourage me to talk about my feelings. He would say, " Baby, don't clam up on me," and "We can talk about anything." I heard the words that were coming out of his mouth, but again I allowed the enemy to make me believe that he didn't really want to talk about my hair loss or my daddy's health issues. My greatest fear was if I told Steve that the doctors don't know if my hair will ever grow back, he wouldn't still want to be my boyfriend. Not only that, but my daddy is dying. I didn't think my dad's health would affect our relationship, but I did think that all of the drama that came along with it would affect it.

In retrospect, I regret not crying more often. I wish I would have thought less of what people would think of me and more about what my true feeling were telling me. Instead, I was trying to protect everyone else's feelings, including those of our church family, people in the community, and relatives.

I told God I was in double trouble! Instead of a double blessing, I would settle for one. My only prayer was for God to heal my daddy. Yes, I wanted my hair to grow back but I felt like I was in a negotiation deal with God. If God wanted to, He could have ended all of this right now. I know that God can handle any and all of our problems. However, the flesh can convince you that God operates like we as humans do. As a result, we start a negotiation process with Him. "Okay, God, if you do this, then you do not have to do that."

Yet, on October 22, 2003, my daddy passed away. I stood at the foot of his bed, wearing my best friend—the wig.

How could a God so full of love, compassion, mercy, and grace be so silent during the darkest days of my life? "God, I begged You; I prayed; I fasted; I sacrificed, I even gave You an option! You are the Almighty, and You did nothing. I'm so *angry* with You that I don't know what to do."

I decided that I was no longer on speaking terms with God. It was like a relationship gone bad, and I ended it with, "I'm not talking to you." I knew in my heart that that wasn't the way to handle my hurt and disappointment, but sometimes things can go so wrong that the only one left to get angry with is God. I couldn't blame anyone else for my condition or my daddy's. No one else could offer a cause and a cure but God. He did neither one.

As we approach the one-year anniversary of my daddy's passing, I can truly say in the words of Patti LaBelle, "I've got a new attitude." God has shown Himself more during this season of grief than at any other time in my life. He has taught me how to better serve others. He has shown His strength, power, and grace in my own life. Most importantly, God continues to remind me that He can do exceedingly, abundantly, above all we can ask or even imagine.

When this journey started, the only question I found myself asking God was, "Why me?" As God slowly began to reveal Himself to me through prayer, reading His Word and different sermons, my question eventually changed. Now I find myself asking God, "Do You trust me enough to go through this suffering?" He shows us in His Word that He has invested in us all we need to endure whatever dark times come our way. He has surrounded us with the people in our lives to encourage us through our tough times.

God's question to us is, "Do you trust me enough to do what I promised?" Do you believe His word in 2 Corinthians 12:9 "My grace is sufficient for thee; for my strength is made perfect in weakness"? When God shows His sustaining power in our lives as we go through suffering and/or grief, He also strengthens us to be able to encourage others during their time of need.

I've found myself growing stronger in this area. By simply being present with another friend or family, I can be a testimony to God's power and shows them if God did it for me, He will do it for you.

In my own life, God has shown me His strength, power, and grace like never before. He's proven that even when the bottom falls from under us, His hands never let us fall. I am a living testimony that God will "Prepare you for what He has prepared for you." I didn't think I would ever truly be happy again, and now I'm happier than I've ever been. I am happy that my daddy is no longer in pain and is now in the place he always preached about. I'm even happier that through my hair loss ordeal, I'm learning to say like Paul, "I've learned that in whatever state I'm in to be content."

In changing my attitude from anger to awesome praise, God has blessed me is so many areas of my life. The most recent and best blessing has been my marriage. God showed his unconditional love for me through my husband, Stephen. God strengthened him to walk along side of me during this long journey. Stephen never once wavered in his love and support for my family and me. I praise God for him and thank God that he gave me my husband at the time he did. He is truly my covering.

And I thank God that, as one pastor has written, "Every hurt is surrounded by a halo, and every cross can be turned into a crown."

SHENIKWA BAILEY-CAGER

UNDER CONSTRUCTION: GOD IS AT WORK!

We never fully realize the special time that we have until time runs out.

That's how I felt when I learned that my father had been diagnosed with a deadly form of cancer. Driving back to my parents' home, I was thinking the entire time, "What could be going on?" About fifteen minutes after everyone was there, Mom, Dad, and Mr. Cunningham pulled up. Dad came in upbeat, trying to establish a somewhat positive atmosphere, but what gave everything away was Mamma. She walked inside the house with her sunglasses on and kept them on.

After they had taken their seats on the couch, I remember someone praying. Immediately Dad started to explain what the doctor had told them. At that point, Mamma told us he had been diagnosed with nasopharyngeal carcinoma and that the doctors gave him the prognosis of the cancer. At that point, everything went quiet. I felt lifeless and drained of all of my energy, like the air inside of me was being pulled out. I proceeded to scan the crowd of people who had gathered in the house. With faces showing disbelief, all were somber and tearful. However, I felt only anger and hatred building inside of me. Basically, one could say that I was angry at God for letting something so devastating happen to my father. One could really say that I broke ties between God and myself. From that day forward, my life began on a downward spiral. In other words, I was on a crash course toward "rock bottom."

Within the next few weeks, he and Mamma took me to school at Lon Morris College in Jacksonville, Texas. Before he left to go to M.D. Anderson in Houston, Texas, Dad told me to "remember where I came from" and to "keep my mind on books." He said, "Don't worry about me. I am going to be all right." I guess he told me that because he knew how much I'm known for worrying and stressing over things that I have no control over. As the semester went on, I just couldn't come to grips with the idea of my father not being here for the next two or three years. The more I thought about it, the more I seemed to fall apart day by day. Also I found myself almost every weekend or every other weekend driving from Morris College to Dallas to pick up my cousins or my play-brother, then to Houston to visit with my mother and father. In a way, I thought I was making up lost time that I didn't spend with him when I was younger. I remember walking out of the bedroom, thinking about all the times he asked me to spend time, and I almost always found some kind of excuse for not doing so.

As I started to see how the treatments took affect on his body, I found myself a lot of nights walking alone around the campus, trying to find some reasons why this was happening to our family. You see it happening to everybody else, and, of course, your heart goes out to that family, but I never thought that it would happen to my family. As God gave answers that I didn't find good enough, I became more and more enraged at people who were trying to say how God is good, and that He would never put any more on us than we could bear. At that time, those were words that I just did not want to hear. But then all of a sudden, everything was over at M. D. Anderson. Everybody was excited.

Dad started doing what he loved best—preaching. He went to Louisiana to preach at his godson's church and also married two couples in various places. The chain of events made me proud to be his son. Here is a man sick and overcoming the odds of what the doctors had said. He even preaches a series on marriage to help the couples at the church.

It seemed that everything was getting back to normal . . . when the cancer started growing, faster and faster. His body started to weaken. It broke my heart to see my dad, this big courageous man, not being able to do the very thing he loved doing the most of all because the cancer had taken over his body. One day he told me, "Son, I would give anything right now to stand up somewhere and preach." This happened after he was not able to stand in the pulpit any longer. That, however, was only the second part of my heart being broken during this whole ordeal. I remember our whole family—Mamma, Kiesha, Sheshe and I sat around the table with Mamma discussing what it would take for all of us to do our share in helping to take care of him. As summer passed and as fall passed, we saw him becoming weaker and weaker.

As 2003 went on, I started thinking this could be the last Christmas that we, as a family, would share with our father. What we did not know was that all of 2003 would be a year of basically nothing but grief for our family. Over a span of several months, Dad tried to find any kind of medicine or treatment that would help slow the cancer down or put it in remission. Yet, everywhere he went, I thought to myself, "God must be with him because he received the utmost respect from everybody he ran into." I never heard of anyone giving him problems when they were giving him treatment. People in different cities went out of their way to help Dad.

Very unexpectedly one morning, Dad's sister called with the message that my granny had died. I could just imagine the pain that added to what Dad was going through. However, during the week of May 3rd, he stood up behind the pulpit of his church, in his weakened condition, and "preached the doors off of the church." He did that for two big funeral services back-to-back. I just could not figure it out. With cancer taking over his body and struggling to get in and out of bed, he still had enough power to stand behind the sacred desk. The most uplifting part about that week was when in the midst of his pain, he made a two-hour trip down to my college and sat through a whole commencement service just to see his son graduate from junior college. When I walked across the stage, I would never forget that big smile going across his face saying, "That's my boy!"

That joy, however, was short lived. He seemed to me to start taking a turn for the worse. I didn't want to believe it; I was in denial of what's going on. In other words, as he began to fade, I began to fade. The faster he went, the faster I went. I remember one day that summer bringing a game of checkers over to their Houston apartment to continue our rivalry in this game. When I went into the room for our game, Dad's pain was so unbearable that he could not play even a simple everyday game such as checkers. At that point, it hit me that the time that I had wasted when I was younger, I would never be able to make up.

And I began to feel like my life was an enormous construction site that had been filled with dirt and rock and building supplies. I could imagine a sign hanging there on my heart that read: *Mandatory hard hats . . . God is at work here!*

One day Mamma called on the cell phone, asking me to hurry to the apartment to help my father. He had tried to get up out of the chair when his legs gave out, she said, and I needed to help get him back into the chair. When I arrived and proceeded to help him into the chair, he grabbed my shirt.

With tears in his eyes, Dad said, "Son, that was the most important thing you could have done to help me." He then pulled me down to him and cried while he embraced me. This was when I finally realized how important I was to him and how much my father really loved me.

As the summer went on, I started watching my father slowly wither away. With God not leading my life, I felt I was headed straight for destruction. Behind all the anger, shame, and guilt, I got to a certain point where I didn't care where my life ended up. Every day seemed darker and darker as Dad slowly started to go through the dying process. I remember the phone calls stating for me to hurry and come to the hospital. One of the worst parts for me was spending week after week going to and from the hospital and sitting all day and almost all night in the hospital room—sleeping in those chairs and in those uncomfortable hospital beds for long periods of time.

Then I was faced with starting the school year at a new school. Shortly after the semester started, I found myself not being able to concentrate on my schoolwork at all. Whenever I would go to class, it seemed like I was not hearing anything that the teacher was saying. All I had on my mind was my father. Eventually it got to a point where I just completely stopped going to school and started staying at the hospital.

One day, in the midst of my being angry with God, He started strengthening me to prepare me for my father's death. Because He allowed this to happen to my father, I didn't want anything to do with Him. One could say that God just reached down and picked me up. I fought Him every way I could, but, as we all know, if God wants to get a hold of you, He can. As Dad got weaker, God began to make me stronger.

Then that day came when I came from school, and Mamma and the doctor said they don't expect Daddy to live through the weekend. I know the doctor was just doing his job, but it took everything inside of me not to get out of my seat and snatch the doctor out of his chair. I wanted to ask him if there was anything else that he could do. In actuality, there was nothing else that we could have done because God was starting to call His servant home to be with Him.

On October 21, 2003, my father was rushed to the hospital. I knew this was probably the last few hours of his life. As I watched what was unfolding, I just couldn't believe that my father was about to leave us forever. I tried to grasp the harsh reality that when he died I would be able to look at his face only in pictures and in my mind. After they had put him into the ambulance, I remember sitting there with face and both hands pressed against the back windows of the ambulance. I found myself beating on the ambulance doors with tears rolling down my face, yelling, "I want my father!" I didn't want to be comforted. I didn't want a pat on the back or a hug, I simply wanted my dad.

At that time, even though his heart was still beating and he was barely breathing, I knew that he was already gone to be with the Lord and that his body was just slowly shutting down. I watched him making his transition from one life to the next. Close friends to the family and staff members from the church started slowly pouring into the hospital. About 2:45 a.m. the crowd of people outside his hospital room started to come two by two into the room and saying their good-byes to him. I guess I just never knew how Daddy was loved by so many people. They showed love to his family just the same. Standing next to his hospital bed in that crowded space that I began to realize that God didn't do this to hurt us. He did it to make us stronger and to help us to grow.

I knew that my father had served his time better than some people had expected him to. He lived for some time with the pain shooting through his body. He lived several months after the doctors thought he would die. He lived joyfully and passionately and he never smothered us with complaints or negative thoughts. He always encouraged us and asked us to rely on Jesus. He made provisions for us in so many ways and he left us in the capable care of his assistant pastor, who would soon become my big brother, mentor, and pastor.

I didn't know what was next for any of us, but the one thing I was sure of was that the church he started and helped build was going to prosper because God had His hands on it . . . and even our family was going to be all right because God had His hands on us too.

Many things can happen to a family that will either make them closer or separate them. God did bring us closer through my father's death. My dad was a man of integrity, faith, character, valor, and stamina, but most of all he was a man who loved to preach the Word of God. He loved laughter, having fun, and cracking jokes, but most importantly, he enjoyed spending time with his family.

I thank God for all that my dad contributed to the lives of my mother, my sisters and me. I know there were times when we didn't always see eye-to-eye, but now I realize that some of those times were just a means for my character and conduct to be shaped by my father's instruction and guidance. He showed me unconditional love—and sometimes even tough love—to discipline me and make me a better person. I thank God that Daddy showed me how to be a man and how I should treat my mother, my sisters, and all women in general. I am grateful that each of us is clinging to God's promises.

Because of our hope in you, Jesus, I know we will see our father again. He wore his "hard hat" for many years and I am so thankful that he passed his "work gear" down to me and my sisters. God was at work then and He is at work now in our lives.

EMON K. BAILEY

REFLECTIONS OF FORMER COLLEAGUES

*S*uffering is never easy. Sometimes it becomes as difficult for friends and loved ones to watch the pain and changes in someone's health as it is for the sufferer to endure the pain and changes. My father was indebted to the entire staff—pastoral and support staff members. He was especially indebted to his assistant pastor, Rev. Bryan Carter, and the executive pastor, Dr. Wright Lassiter, for guiding our church at such a crucial time. He was so grateful for the individuals who worked in his office to keep things going. His illness affected them in many ways, but they kept pushing.

It is with great love and respect that he asked that I highlight and recognize the efforts of all of the staff members, elders, deacons, and leaders of Concord. Here are remembrances from just some of the staff.

ANGEL HERNANDEZ,
Office Assistant

Pastor was more to me than just a supervisor. He was my friend, confidant, and "other father." We teased one another and shared many laughs, but when it was time to get back to business, we were able to put on our professional hats. When I joined Concord, I had been involved in church, but I had not entered into a deep and intimate relationship with Jesus. Because Pastor Bailey spent time teaching me one-on-one, I learned how to view Christ as my own personal companion.

Life-changing is the word that comes to mind when I think about his impact on my life. Because I have known him and watched him, my life will not be the same.

I have never been around anybody before who had cancer. It broke my heart to see what Pastor Bailey had to go through. I just didn't want him to have to suffer.

Watching him battle cancer increased my prayer life. When he first got sick, I went into the prayer room faithfully with Elder Rick Jordan, calling out Pastor Bailey's name. I found myself praying at all times for Pastor Bailey. My prayer life went to new levels. I felt myself feeling sad, but I knew what God was capable of doing in his life. I knew that Pastor did not need pity, so I prayed and became convicted that God allowed Pastor to suffer so that people could do what God was asking of them.

This cancer, I believe, was not for him but for the church. I think we did not really get on board for the first cancer, and God said, "I know how I can get your attention. I'll let him suffer again until you get on board." Suffering is another level that one must go through. I have heard that God cannot use people until they suffer. I don't think that a person is able to go to the next level without suffering. His suffering has helped me to view painful times in my life differently.

His faith got stronger and mine did too. I don't think that one can really live without faith, and Pastor Bailey brought that home in his walk. I saw how he still made time for the important things in life and remained both positive and optimistic.

Now, a year later, I find myself still drawing from his courageous example. I want to reflect the character and the hope that he displayed continually.

In the time that I served Pastor Bailey, when he was at full strength and when he had reached his weakest state, I never saw him drowning in despair. He kept his head lifted up and he encouraged us to do the same. When he came to service one evening wrapped up in a blanket with gloves on, he was the best image of hope and commitment that I had ever seen. If cancer couldn't stop him from worshiping and entering God's house, then the rest of us don't have an excuse.

My children and I are more committed because God used Pastor Bailey to shape our lives and to mold our faith.

BRYAN CARTER
Pastor

My relationship with Pastor Bailey was multidimensional. I considered it a privilege to be part of a father/son, teacher/apprentice, and teacher/student relationship. Since our first meeting, he continuously taught me what a father teaches a son and what a senior pastor teaches a young minister.

What I appreciated most about Pastor Bailey is that he was such a model. He didn't force me to be like him, but he allowed me to be myself. He opened his heart and allowed me to come in.

As I thought about his suffering, I was amazed. Prior to Pastor's experience, I didn't believe suffering was truly of God. I had an idea, but I still struggled with the source of suffering. After this experience, I gained a greater appreciation for suffering. Suffering is a part of misery on the inside. Prior to the diagnosis, I said to him, "Do we always cause our own suffering?" He responsed by describing the difference between the crop and the cross.

"Your crop is the suffering you experience through the seeds that you plant," he said. "The cross is the suffering that you receive when you go to the cross and stay there." I believed suffering was something I had to go through because of making wrong choices or because I had to suffer for Christ. I now see the cross as a willingness to go through suffering in a way that glorifies God.

I remember feeling intense anxiety sitting in Pastor's living room when he told us about cancer in the nasal passage. The elders were there, and I felt scared—scared because of the nature of the illness. He calmed a lot of the fears as he began to share truths from his life and from Scripture. I remember him sharing that whomever God uses greatly has to be hurt significantly.

"I have been trusting God too long not to practice what I preach," he said. I saw him living his faith and calming my fears with his faith.

Now my own challenges are in perspective because he believed God was faithful. Pastor Bailey even encouraged me by saying, "Young prophet, you are destined to be a spiritual all star." I didn't know what he meant, but I felt encouraged to know he had confidence in me and allowed me to lead our group in prayer.

God would allow his illness to grow me, Pastor explained. He allowed me to preach on several occasions in his stead while he was ill; that was intimidating at times, but God used him to help me to gain assertiveness and confidence in Christ.

Now that he is not with us, we keep his core values alive and strive to be the church that God has created us to be. That's what Pastor Bailey would desire. As he shared with me that God wanted me to be the next pastor, I thought it to be a tremendous privilege and responsibility. I also felt a little bit of everything—from fear and trembling to joy and awe. I don't think I really comprehended it. It's not something I could plan for or pray for. I remember thinking, *God, are you sure?*

For the most part, I just say to myself, *God, You know what You are doing, so I trust You.* I won't try to fill Pastor Bailey's shoes. I could never fit those shoes, but I am committed to doing what I promised him that I would and that is to lead God's people faithfully for this season.

If there was one thing I learned from our pastor, it was the importance of having a growing relationship with the Lord. He taught me to have a passion for a consistent diet of the Word of God and for cooperating with the Holy Spirit as it changes me daily. His cancer battle only refined him as a man of God, and I praise God for the privilege to witness his incredible model!

. LAWRENCE AKER
Research Assistant

Dr. Bailey lived for a good fight. Battling cancer would be his ultimate fight. When he first told me he had cancer, in 1997, it was a somber conversation that turned hopeful. He told me that the doctor would perform surgery, and following his recovery everything should return to normal. This would be my initial insight into Pastor's suffering. I recall hearing him two years later in the pulpit describing his new revelation on an old hymn "Great Is Thy Faithfulness." He revealed that the words meant more to him since he had learned to live with a recurring pain in his side.

The once relaxing times following his sermons would now forever be replaced with moments when he would grimace with pain, while rubbing the side where the surgeon's scalpel had been applied. He would still laugh and compare past days when he could preach all week, jump on an airplane, and commence a citywide revival elsewhere with minimal effort. The new Pastor Bailey began to teach lessons on living with pain.

Nevertheless, my biggest lesson came when I first saw him wheelchair-bound, in the summer of 2002. Since my family and I were doing ministry in New York, we communicated on the phone. Sure his voice sounded weaker than my ministry supervisor of the early nineties, but an image was frozen in my mind of a commander. I had worked with Dr. Bailey as his preaching research assistant from 1991 to 1995, while attending Dallas Theological Seminary. My time was spent poring through periodicals, magazines, newspapers, commentaries, and library stacks. However, the combination of excellence and life lessons padded the curriculum.

Dr. Bailey had no problem working into the wee hours of the morning—and keeping you up with him. He would constantly remind me, "Lawrence, losers go to bed with their work undone on Saturday nights, but winners do whatever it takes."

Now, in 2002, I knew he was spending more time searching for specialists, but I felt that was just a precautionary measure. Yet when we met and he rolled himself into the room, I saw another side of his indomitable strength. He broke the silence, saying, "Well, don't just stand there, young prophet, give me a hug!" I learned on the spot never to give up or succumb to adversity. Although his life had been altered, he absolutely refused to give up.

What lesson does E. K. Bailey teach the world? One word for me: *press*. That's what he would often tell me. Simply yet powerfully press your way through and continue to strive regardless of what you face, hear, see, feel, fear, or dread. His unwavering dependence and trust in the Lord has been transferred to me. What my family already instilled within me, God used Dr. Bailey to profoundly stir up.

I hope those who cherish Dr. Bailey's legacy will internalize his press. As he entitled one of his classic sermons, it is always "Too Soon to Quit." We must all press beyond our circumstances because "great is His faithfulness."

Appendix

THE BEGINNING
TO AN END

Heart Questions for
the Patient and Caregiver

*W*hether you are a patient, spouse, caregiver, child, relative, or friend, how would you classify your heart pain—the level of loss and hurt you feel for the loved one who is suffering now? On a scale of 1 to 10, circle the extent of your pain. Let 10 equal very intense and 1 equal everything is okay (denial).

10   9   8   7   6   5   4   3   2   1

Check the assets you have for your crisis:

❏ A personal relationship with Jesus

❏ Medical background

❏ Perseverance (a willingness to hang in there)

❏ Contact with people in medicine

- ☐ Organizational skills
- ☐ Loving attitude
- ☐ Physical strength
- ☐ Nutritional experience
- ☐ Each other
- ☐ Insurance
- ☐ Long-term health insurance
- ☐ Family
- ☐ Willingness to adapt

If you are married, discuss this assessment of yourself with your spouse. It wouldn't be a bad idea if your spouse or other family members also take this assessment.

Check the liabilities you have for your crisis:

- ☐ Have not accepted Jesus Christ as Savior, therefore cannot stand on His promises
- ☐ Fear
- ☐ No insurance
- ☐ Lack of people support
- ☐ Poor communication
- ☐ Lack of transparency (do not trust others with information about the illness)

If you are the patient, what is important to you and causing the greatest fear(s)?

- ☐ Becoming healthy
- ☐ That I will suffer greatly
- ☐ Being unable to watch my children grow up
- ☐ My career
- ☐ That my spouse may not accept me

If you are a spouse, caregiver, child, relative, or friend, what is causing the greatest fear(s)?

- ☐ That the patient will die
- ☐ That he or she will suffer greatly
- ☐ That he or she will not see the children grow up nor give love and support

Here are four ways to turn your liabilities into your assets:

1. Accept the Lord Jesus as your Savior. (See Romans 10:9–10.) Focus on one issue at a time, being transformed by the Spirit of God.

2. Develop a plan.

3. Be accountable to someone.

4. Believe that God keeps His promises.

ACKNOWLEDGMENTS

*M*any thanks are due for the completion of this project, and they begin with my wife. Thank you to my friend, ministry partner, and confidant, Mrs. Sheila M. Bailey. Truly this project would have never been completed if you were not by my side, rooting and cheering for its success. I pray that the Lord will allow me to see this book published, but if He chooses to call me home, I am sure that you will pray, write, and administrate to the glory of God.

Thank you for input and investment into this project. Thank you for opening up your heart to the world as they hear our journey of hope. Thank you for dreaming for me and with me. Because of God's abiding love and your ministry of presence, I have never been alone. I love you.

To my daughter Cokiesha, whom I have watched as she has developed into an excellent writer and inquisitive student of the Word. Thank you for agreeing to tackle this project with me. When they told me that I could choose any writer, I had only one choice—you. Thank you for writing this cancer story with such passion. I have always trusted your heart with my words. I'm grateful that you believed in this project when it was only an idea. Thanks for making it happen. I am so proud of you.

Thank you to my youngest daughter, Shenikwa, and my son, Emon. Our family has ministered together for many years, and we have learned, by God's grace, how to balance ministry and family. You have helped me to know when to be Daddy, when to be pastor, and when to be friend and confidant. Thank you for loving me and for encouraging us as we tell the story. Your valuable insight and contributions to this book will not only give cancer patients and their families a glimpse of your hearts, but it will show people the indelible impression that an illness can have on the lives of their family members. I honor you for your boldness.

My sincere thanks to the Moody Publishers staff. Larry Mercer and Greg Thornton, you have played such a valuable role in making this project a reality. Your insight, listening ear, prayers, and trips to Dallas to just sit and talk have encouraged me. Your sensitivity to my emotional needs and those of my family members has really been a blessing to each of us. Thank you for being men whom God can use. Most of all, thank you for being my friends.

Thank you, Hansel Cunningham, for being a man after God's own heart. Words cannot adequately convey my heartfelt appreciation to you and your family for all of the sacrifices you are making during my illness. I have never seen a man who shows love more freely than you. You have been an accountability partner, a motivator, an encourager, and Sheila's and my right-hand man. We're indebted to you. This story would be incomplete without you. Thanks for helping us make it happen.

My thanks to Felix Spencer, Brenton Cross, Dixie Daughtry, Cassandra Anderson, and Malcolm and Elaine Hoard for your caring spirits and helpful hands. Your assistance in our home helped us move forward on this book and in our daily lives. You have blessed us more than we could ever say.

To Myron Hardy who worked so diligently to help me organize thoughts and ideas for this book, thanks. My brother. Our brainstorming sessions and your diligent labor helped to build a blueprint for us to develop.

Special thanks to Dorothy Robinson, my friend and longtime church member who came out of retirement to assist in completing this special project. I couldn't imagine this book without your seal of excellence. Thanks for always serving with a "Yes, I'll be happy to" spirit. You have always been counted on, and I thank you for your commitment, loyalty, and editorial eye.

Thank you to Mrs. Cheryl Thompson for keeping me organized and uplifted. You have impacted my life with your tremendous gifts and your service to me and my family. Thank you for bringing our church's core values to life through your work and tireless spirit. You and John have blessed us beyond measure.

To Ms. Angel Hernandez, thank you for being a liaison to us as we have been communicating in several different cities. Your helpful hands, charismatic spirit, and hearty laughter have been a remarkable blessing to us. Thanks for always sacrificing and for serving beyond the call of duty.

We are grateful to Hope Hogan who has always made herself available to our family. Thank you for helping us as we gathered information, edited, and passed it from one hand to another. Your speed and typing skills continue to astonish us.

Thanks to Bryan Carter, who brings breadth and depth to everything he does. Thank you for agreeing to lead Concord whenever the Lord chooses to take me home. Your commitment to God and to your calling has blessed me. Thank you for coming alongside me and helping me to "move the ship forward." I would not have been able to do this project if you were not working so diligently with our staff and leaders, our members, and our family. Thank you for your investment in this book and into my life. You and Stephanie are exceeding our expectations as you both serve so humbly and enthusiastically as members of our pastoral and ministers' wives team.

My thanks to Tracie Cavitt for jumping in the saddle with us. Your commitment to excellence on every level has been an asset to our staff. Thanks for being available to us as we worked on this project.

I appreciate the entire pastoral and administrative staff, elders, and deacons at Concord for being eager to serve, administrate, and render support. Thank you for trusting me as your leader and for being trustworthy individuals. You have remained diligent, compassionate, and caring as we have transitioned because of my health challenges. I am able to tell my story because you have gone farther in and deeper down with me.

I also appreciate Pastor Rodney Stodghill for investing his wisdom in this project. Thank you for helping Sheila, me, and our children to "heart hold one another." We appreciate how you've taught our church how to caringly cope with one another as we deal with sickness, transition, death, and grief. Now, we can see Jesus standing behind us.

I am indebted to Willie Richardson, Leroy Armstrong, and Aquila Allen, who stepped up to the plate as friends and colaborers and assisted me in giving leadership to the E. K. Bailey International Expository Preaching Conference each year. I am able to write and recuperate because you are faithful to the cause. Thank you for your loyalty and consistency in serving others.

Melvin V. and Jacquie G. Wade epitomize Christian friendship, and I thank both of you for keeping a bright smile on our faces as we are pressing toward the mark. You have been consistent in showing us love and support for more than thirty years. Your friendship is a rare gift that we cherish.

Thanks to Pastor and Mrs. S. J. Gilbert and Pastor and Mrs. Ross Cullins and Pastor and Mrs. A. L. Patterson for being Sheila and my prayer partners. We cannot begin to tell you how your prayers refreshed us time and time again.

To all of the dynamic pastors around the country who came to preach at Concord while I was away from the pulpit, thank you. I am able to rest, write, and recover because of your sacrificial service. Your friendship humbles me.

I must also acknowledge some professionals who also have made this book possible: the doctors who have worked so hard to provide me with quality care. I thank God for your professionalism and for your ability to bring care, concern, and coping strategies to the table.

Finally, some close members and friends of the family:

- My sister, Vivian Flakes, and my sister-in-law, Dorothy Bailey, who have worked so hard to assist Sheila in caring for me. Thank you for being compassionate caregivers and faithful sisters to me and my wife.

- My longtime friend, Dr. Robert Smith, whom I have admired and respected for many years. I am humbled that you would participate in this project. Thank you for releasing the fragrance of Jesus Christ with your life. You inspired this book.

- Our "other children," Katina, Tan, Alicia, Yomica, Shelley, and Racquel. Thank you for sticking with us during all of our runs to the hospital and even late night at the house. You motivated me to write—even on bad days. Thanks for loving our family. Your energy always sparked a flame in my heart that made me want to run on.

Thank you to Rick and Sandra Jordan who served us faithfully. You both are more than sister-in-law and brother-in-law to me; you all are loving neighbors and faithful friends who make my load easier to bear.

Thank you to Elder Rick and Brother Cedric Jordan and the entire Prayer Team that orchestrated prayer teams to cover me and my family around the clock throughout this journey. Your faithfulness will never be forgotten. Our church went to another level in prayer because of your efforts.

Thanks to Dr. and Mrs. Timothy Winters for making a place available to the family to write and retreat. And thanks to Detra Kelly and B. J. Bass for helping to make our house a home while we were getting treatment.

And thank you to the members of Concord Church and all the friends, family members, and believers around the world who contributed to this story by praying, hoping, and displaying love in a myriad of ways.

DR. E. K. BAILEY, founder of the Concord Missionary Baptist Church, Dallas TX, went to be with the Lord in October 2003. During his illustrious tenure as pastor he began sponsoring the Institute on Church Growth Conference in 1982 to help African American Churches improve their administrative and Christian operations through shared leadership. The focus was on how to develop a biblical philosophy of ministry, and how to put that which was learned into practice. From this concept, E. K. Bailey Ministries, Inc., 501(c)(3) was originally founded in 1989 with a mission to provide the basic principles and practices of biblical church growth to African American pastors. However, through Dr. Bailey's visionary leadership EKBM became a beacon for racial reconciliation and interdenominational ministry. These values instilled by Dr. Bailey exist today and continue to be developed and expanded through EKBM where his wife, Dr. Sheila M. Bailey, is the president.

<u>THE MISSION</u>:
The mission of E. K. Bailey Ministries is to provide principles and practices of Biblical Church health to pastors, preachers, and leaders in order to empower the Church to impact the world for Christ and His kingdom.

CONTACT INFO:
E. K. Bailey Ministries, Inc.
P. O. Box 764679
Dallas, TX 75376-4679

PHONE: 1-800-933-8067
PHONE (local): 972-708-9979
FAX: 972-708-9985

E-MAIL: ekbmhears@aol.com
ONLINE: www.ekbailey.org

FARTHER IN AND DEEPER DOWN TEAM

ACQUIRING EDITOR
Greg Thornton

COPY EDITOR
Jim Vincent

BACK COVER COPY
Smartt Guys

COVER DESIGN
Smartt Guys

COVER PHOTO
Mary Ann Sherman, Sherman Studios

INTERIOR DESIGN
Paetzold Associates

PRINTING AND BINDING
Quebecor World Book Services

The typeface for the text of this book is
Berkeley